The Actor in Costume

'This lively, ambitious, and readable
element in the understanding and in
much more than a treatment of costu.... .... *The Actor in Costume* makes an immediate difference to our thinking about performance today.' – W. B. Worthen, *Alice Brady Pels Professor in the Arts, Barnard College, Columbia University, USA.*

How do audiences look at actors in costume onstage? How does costume shape theatrical identity and form bodies? What do audiences wear to the theatre? This lively and cutting-edge book explores these questions, and engages with the various theoretical approaches to the study of actors in performance. Aoife Monks focuses in particular on the uncanny ways in which costume and the actor's body are indistinguishable in the audience's experience of a performance.

From the role of costume in Modernist theatre to the actor's position in the fashion system, from nudity to stage ghosts, this wide-ranging exploration of costume and its histories argues for the centrality of costume to the spectator's experience at the theatre. Drawing on examples from paintings, photographs, live performances, novels, reviews, blogs and plays, Monks presents a vibrant analysis of the very peculiar work that actors and costumes do on the stage.

Aoife Monks is a Lecturer in Theatre Studies at Birkbeck College, University of London. She has published on the work of the Wooster Group and Deborah Warner and global performances of Irishness.

The Actor in Costume

Aoife Monks

First published 2010 by
PALGRAVE MACMILLAN

Palgrave Macmillan in the UK is an imprint of Macmillan Publishers Limited, registered in England, company number 785998, of Houndmills, Basingstoke, Hampshire RG21 6XS.

Palgrave Macmillan in the US is a division of St Martin's Press LLC, 175 Fifth Avenue, New York, NY 10010.

Palgrave Macmillan is the global academic imprint of the above companies and has companies and representatives throughout the world.

Palgrave® and Macmillan® are registered trademarks in the United States, the United Kingdom, Europe and other countries.

ISBN-13: 978-0-230-21699-0 hardback
ISBN-13: 978-0-230-21700-3 paperback

This book is printed on paper suitable for recycling and made from fully managed and sustained forest sources. Logging, pulping and manufacturing processes are expected to conform to the environmental regulations of the country of origin.

A catalogue record for this book is available from the British Library.

A catalog record for this book is available from the Library of Congress.

10   9   8   7   6   5   4   3   2   1
19 18 17 16 15 14 13 12 11 10

Printed and bound in Great Britain by
CPI Antony Rowe, Chippenham and Eastbourne

To my parents, who gave me my first box of dressing-up clothes and have regretted it ever since

Contents

List of Illustrations

Acknowledgements

This book has been long in the making and I owe many people thanks for their help along the way. Of course, my colleagues, and friends at Trinity College Dublin, most of all Anna McMullan and Matthew Causey whose supervision and support made much of the early stages of the work for this book in the form of my doctoral thesis possible, as did funding and support from the Government of Ireland postgraduate scholarship scheme. Huge thanks are also due to the participants of the International Centre for Advanced Studies in Finland, the Scuddlist, and the Feminism and Theatre working Group at IFTR. My colleagues at Reading and Birkbeck, particularly Teresa Murjas, Tom Healy, Helen Freshwater, Rob Swain, Michael Dobson and Andrew McKinnon have offered me homes for thinking about theatre. An Arts Faculty research grant made it possible for me to extend my research leave to complete this book, for which I am hugely grateful. I spoke to a number of artists: Sam West, Tina Bicat, Lez Brotherstone, Mick Barnfather, Fiona Shaw, Deborah Warner and members of The Wooster Group about costume, and their generous responses have informed, directly or indirectly, the work here. The London Theatre Seminar was the first place I aired my approach to costume, and I want to thank its many excellent participants, most of all Joe Kelleher who painstakingly read this material in its nascent and chaotic stages and whose advice was crucial for reshaping, rethinking and redressing this book. Equally, the feedback from Bridget Escolme and Bill Worthen was essential for the book's development. The team at Palgrave Macmillan have been unerring in their support. Finally, many thanks are due to my friends and family who have been nothing but supportive, and this of course includes Russell Celyn Jones whose story about the pantomime dame in Swansea didn't quite make it into my discussion – until now – but this story, and his many others, have sustained me through writing this book.

The author and publishers wish to thank the following for permission to reproduce copyright material:

Images

Richard Campbell for an image from National Theatre of Scotland's *The Bacchae*, (www.richardcampbell.co.uk).

Stuart Pearson Wright for 'Sir Michael Gambon as Sir John Falstaff at the National Theatre 2005' (www.stuartpearsonwright.com).

The Norton Simon Foundation for Edgar Degas' 'Actress in Her Dressing Room'.

The Samuel Courtauld Trust, Courtauld Gallery, London, for Renoir's 'La Loge'.

Harry Ransom Humanities Research Center, The University of Texas at Austin for 'Joseph Murphy cross-dressed'.

The Folger Shakespeare Library for Ducarme's 'Garrick. tragédien Anglais ne en 1716, mort en 1779. (Rôle d'Hamlet.) Galerie Universelle. publiee par Blaisot.'

Hugo Glendinning and Forced Entertainment for an image from Forced Entertainment's *Bloody Mess* (2004).

Extracts

Penguin Books Ltd for extracts from Euripides, trans. Philip Vellacott, *The Bacchae and Other Plays* (Penguin 1954, Revised 1972, pp. 225–5).

The Society of Authors, on behalf of the Bernard Shaw Estate for extracts pp. 51, 61–62, 114 from *Major Barbara* (Penguin, 1957).

Faber and Faber for extracts pp. 95, 146 from Norman and Stoppard's *Shakespeare In Love* (Faber and Faber, 1999).

Yale University for extracts pp. 116, 118, 119, 145 from Eugene O'Neill's *The Emperor Jones* (Signet Classics, 1998).

Forced Entertainment for quotes from their productions of *Bloody Mess* (2004) and *Spectacular* (2008).

The West End Whingers for extracts from their review of *Equus with Daniel Radcliffe* (http://westendwhingers.wordpress.com/2007/03/20/review-equus-with-daniel-radcliffe/).

Introduction: The Dress Rehearsal

Euripides' *The Bacchae* is a play about the dangers of dressing-up. The god Dionysus punishes the people of Thebes for refusing to acknowledge him. He sends the women of the city mad, and turns them into his worshippers: the Bacchants. Dionysus' punishment is particularly harsh for Pentheus, the ruler of Thebes, who attempts to eject him from the city. Dionysus teaches Pentheus a lesson by telling him that the only way he can spy on his mother, Agave, and the other Bacchants, is by dressing up as a woman. In his eagerness to watch the women unobserved, Pentheus agrees to cross-dress. He climbs into a tree to spy on the women but falls, and mistaking him for a lion cub, the women tear him apart. Agave triumphantly carries his head back to the city, whereupon she discovers that she is looking into the dismembered face of her own son.

Pentheus changes his dress purely in order to spy on his mother, but finds that his sight has been transformed once he is dressed in the robes and wig of a woman. He sees Dionysus in animal form: 'You are a bull I see leading me forward now; a pair of horns seems to have grown upon your head' (Euripides, 1954, p. 225). And his vision begins to blur: 'why now! I seem to see two suns; a double Thebes' (Euripides, 1954, p. 224). Dressing-up makes Pentheus see double. Perhaps this is not so surprising; after all, Dionysus is the god of wine and theatre. It turns out that dressing-up has made Pentheus drunk, disorienting him, allowing him to access versions of the world previously unavailable to him, and he is liberated from his rigid masculinity. His transformation is not necessarily benign, however. Dressing-up destroys Pentheus: it leads to his death. The play suggests that costuming is both dangerous and restorative, but fundamentally necessary for the health of the social order.

Euripides' play uses the work of the actor as a metaphor for identity. After all, while Pentheus wants to be a spectator in his desire to watch the women of Thebes unobserved, he finds that he must mimic another sex in order to do so, just as actors did on the Greek stage. Pentheus turns into an actor in the hopes of becoming an audience member. As a result, the moment in the play when Pentheus changes his clothes closely resembles a dress rehearsal, a scene largely (and comically) centred on his attempts to make his performance as a woman convincing. Dionysus and Pentheus rehearse his impersonation, checking that his use of costume and gesture are correct, with Pentheus asking: 'how do I look? Tell me, is not the way I stand [...] like my mother Agave?' (Euripides, 1954, p. 225). When Dionysus chides: 'here a curl has slipped out of its proper place,' Pentheus replies, 'indoors, as I was tossing my head up and down like a Bacchic dancer, I dislodged it from its place' (Euripides, 1954, p. 225). Here we see an actor trying to get his performance right: attempting to ensure that his hair, and dress and gestures will make his audience believe that what they see is the real thing. Of course, what Pentheus risks in getting his performance wrong, in failing to convince, is death rather than lacklustre applause or booing. But perhaps Pentheus risks literally what the actor risks psychically: the possibility of "corpsing" or "dying" onstage when failing to convince (see Ridout, 2006, p. 135). Dress rehearsals are necessitated by the risks and possibilities of dressing-up.

There might have been another form of double vision at work in this scene when an audience first saw the play performed in Ancient Greece. I'd like to imagine that when the audience saw Dionysus and Pentheus they also saw, doubly, the masked actors playing those roles. Of course, it's impossible to know what they "really saw", since the first performance was around 2500 years ago, and we can never really know how spectators see a performance anyway. However, I'd like to think that when Pentheus dressed up in women's clothes, the audience were aware that they were watching a double dressing: an actor dressed up as Pentheus dressing up as a woman. Similarly, when Agave entered the stage at the end of the play, holding Pentheus's head, the audience might have also seen a male actor in a "female" mask, carrying the empty mask of Pentheus. The mask continues to represent the character, but its emptiness is at the heart of its lifelessness (see Peter Arnott, 1959). Furthermore, the empty mask draws attention to the fact that the other actors are also wearing masks, that masks are distinct, and yet not distinct, from the bodies that wear them. As Charles Segal argues: 'once we are made to feel that a mask is a mask, that a character before us is an actor, not "Pentheus", "Agave" or "Dionysus" we exchange the sense of pure presence for a double vision' (Segal, 1982, p. 239). The presence of actors as not-character emerges when a mask is used without an actor in it: the mask stands as a memory of the body that occupied it, and makes both actors and masks seem momentarily very strange indeed. In this moment, just like Pentheus, the audience experience double vision when watching the play. In their attempts to watch unobserved, they are forced to see doubly and disorientingly at the theatre.

This is a book about the double visions engendered by the act of dressing-up at the theatre. It is about "costuming" rather than "costume": not about dress, but rather about its uses, perception and effects in the relations between the actor, the costume and the audience. Costuming might be read as a verb rather than as a noun therefore: an act or event that is centred on the ways in which audiences look at an actor dressed up onstage. After all, to talk about costume in distinction from the actor and the audience, we would have to speak about a bunch of dead fabric on a hanger, or think of the actor as a living paper doll. To separate actors from their costumes fails to do justice to the incredibly complex act of looking that an audience must do when watching Pentheus dressing up. His plight suggests that costume does far more than decorate the surface of the body; rather, that it comes with risks and possibilities for the bodies and psyches of actor and audience alike. Pentheus stands as a reminder of the interaction between how we see the world, and what we wear. It is difficult, if not impossible therefore, to establish clear distinctions between actors and their clothes (or indeed between real life and the stage), and this book will make no attempt to do so. Instead, it examines the porous relations between actor and costume and audience, by thinking about dressing-up at the theatre.

In fact, it's in the porousness between actors and their costumes, and between life and performance, where the interest in costuming lies. By thinking about costuming we can imagine theatre as a contradictory place of illusion where audiences can look at real clothes. We can think about the dress of the audience and the actor, and consider the actor's role in the fashion system. We can consider the power of costuming to shape identity and form bodies. Costuming can also invoke the audience's deeply complicated act of looking at the surface of the actor's body, and allows us recognise how the performance might not want us to "see" the actor's surface, but rather encourage us to look beyond, past, or through it to some imaginary internal substance or being. And of course, costuming, like Pentheus's dismembered mask, also reminds us of how very strange the theatrical experience can be. All of these possibilities are historically contingent and require that we think about specific actors, costumes and audiences, in particular places, at one performance rather than another.

Approaches to Costume

Of course, in order to account for the various effects, meanings and functions of costuming, we need to consider it from a number of angles. If we could freeze a moment between Pentheus and Dionysus onstage, we might walk around it and ask a number of questions about its effects. This

Figure 1   Tony Curran (L) and Alan Cumming (R) in The National Theatre of Scotland's production of The Bacchae (Richard Campbell, photograph, 2007, by permission of Richard Campbell).

photograph from the National Theatre of Scotland's production at the Edinburgh Festival from 2007 might help us to be specific (see Figure 1). Here we see the actor Alan Cumming, known for his film roles (not least the baddie in a James Bond movie), playing Dionysus in a black curly wig, a gold lame waistcoat and skirt, and white make-up. Pentheus, played by Tony Curran, wears a black contemporary suit (this is an image from earlier on in the play, before Pentheus cross dresses). Cumming as Dionysus is standing, bound at the wrists, while Pentheus touches his face in an act that might be read at once as desirous and threatening. Of course, this is a photograph, not a performance, and as such, it can't be taken as representative of "what really happened" in the production. The photograph might instead be seen as a faulty memory of the performance, and its stillness allows us to artificially slow down the moment, and to look at it in isolation, in order to imagine its possible meanings.

We might want to ask about the historical context of the image – when and where it was taken, and what was taking place in the wider culture – in order to help us understand what the performance might have meant for its spectators. We might ask about the effects on Cumming and Curran, and whether they felt transformed (like Pentheus) by the costumes they wore. We could ask about the relationship between the stage costumes and the audience's dress (were some men in the audience dressed like Curran for example, and how did they then feel when he put on a dress?), and consider the relationship between the costuming and the fashion system. We might ask whether these costumes were beautiful, and how we might find out if they were beautiful by considering their role in the aesthetic logic of the performance (we might also wonder what the purpose of their beauty might be). We could ask how these costumes imagined identity: what did the cross-dressing of Pentheus *and* Dionysus mean for the audience? What gendered and sexual relations did the performances enact and how did costume make those enactments possible? We could ask what the costumes did to the audience's sense of the actor's presence, whether, in the case of Cumming, they prioritised the character of Dionysus, or Cumming's virtuosity, or his star status (was the Bond villain a part of the audience's experience of Dionysus?). We might ask what the costumes did to the audience's sense of the actors' bodies: what did they imagine the actors looked like without costumes on? We could ask how memories of previous roles and performances informed the design of costumes and how the spectator made sense of the performance. We might also want to think about the strangeness of the costumes, how they might have occasionally reminded the audience of the distinction between actor and role, or indeed of the uncanniness of the theatre event more generally. And, we might ask what happened to the costumes when the show ended, and what they would look like without Alan Cumming and Tony Curran in them.

Answering each of these questions would tell us something different about costuming. Rather than suggesting that costuming has one primary set of effects or meanings, walking around this image shows us how history and context inform the operations of the image and, equally, how our own agenda, when approaching the image, may inflect its meanings. This book takes a wide range of approaches to the study of costume. So, along with walking around this image of Pentheus and Dionysus, and asking questions about its meanings and effects, we might also walk around it and consider the different ways we might approach the image, the different sorts of considerations we might need to take into account when thinking through the implications of costuming in this photograph.

For example, we could take a semiotic approach to the costuming, looking at the interlocking structures of meaning within the individual costumes, and between the costumes and their relationship with other systems of meaning on the stage. We might, for example, consider how Alan Cumming's gold lame outfit relates to his black curly wig, and to his make-up, and furthermore, how the design of his costume was made meaningful by the actor's gesture and movement, and by the scenographic design for the production. In other words, we might trace the audience's experience of the production by looking at how meaning happens *in between* the costume and the actor's gestures, or in between the costumed actor and the lights, and so on. Meaning takes place within a web of signifiers then, and the significance of the gold lame dress can't be completely fixed, rather its meanings shift continually depending on its relation to the other elements of the performance. The audience are in a constant state of flux therefore: their engagement with the costume shifts continuously within this flickering system of meanings. Fundamentally, audience can never access the absolutely "true" meaning of the gold costume: given that meaning keeps shifting through the shifting relations of performance elements, its significance is fundamentally arbitrary, and is produced by the complex set of relations within the theatre event (see Martin Esslin, 1978).

However, the semiotic approach doesn't seem to cater adequately for the strangeness of Pentheus's disembodied mask at the end of the Greek performance. After all, a semiotic approach assumes that we look at costume to see beyond it, to its meanings and significance for the production. But, sometimes costume remains stubbornly in view *as* costume, refusing to be meaningful, or exerting a power beyond its role in the fictional event. If Agave tripped and dropped the mask accidentally, for example, the spectator's response might be to see Pentheus's head being dropped, or they might experience a sudden interruption of the illusion, and feel that the "real" action of dropping the mask had pierced the frame of the performance and suddenly rendered the mask stubbornly present as an object onstage. This is what I am suggesting of the strangeness of the mask in the first place: when we watch this final scene we see doubly, Agave holding the head of her son, and a masked actor holding an empty mask, an object that is eerie and odd and has a power beyond its role in the fiction.

Bert States suggests that this effect of oddness always takes place in the theatre when dogs appear onstage: 'here we have a case in which strangeness, for both actor and audience, can be the occasion of either nervousness or delight. [...] In short, we have a real dog on an artificial street' (States, 1985, p. 33). Later in this book I will argue that our perception of the presence of the "real" in the theatre tends to be an outcome of the performance, rather than being distinct from it, and we can see in the case of Pentheus's mask, or the appearance of the dog, instances in which spectators feel they are in the presence of a "real" object that does strange things to their experience of the performance, but which is actually an outcome of the illusion. When we walk around the image of *The Bacchae*, then, we don't only look for meanings; we might also want to account for the oddness and discomfort that the costume might create through the perception of its stubborn presence in performance.

So far we've accounted for how the spectator might think and feel about the costume they see in this image of *The Bacchae*, but we haven't accounted for the ways in which the spectator's own agendas, contexts and histories might influence *how* they think and feel. After all, a five-year-old girl is unlikely to view Cumming dancing in his gold lame outfit in the same way as a 56-year-old right-wing homophobic woman, or a 20-year-old drag queen might. The five-year-old might be reminded of her Barbie doll, the homophobe might feel intensely uncomfortable at the image, and a drag queen might wonder where Cumming got his skirt. The audience's prior experience and knowledge of theatre, their socio-economic context, and the context and conditions of the theatre event itself are factors that will inform their relationship with the costume's possible meanings, suggesting that the effects costuming cannot take place until they interact with the actor in costume.

Furthermore, we can see in this image that costuming is situated within a wider set of social power relations. This image might be understood by somebody who hasn't seen the play as a depiction, or even assertion, of homophobia: we see a man in a suit possibly threaten a man in a dress. The fact that Pentheus will go on to cross dress, and be killed for it, can be understood in relation to the social myths and stereotypes of the wider culture of Ancient Greece and/or contemporary Scotland. However, it isn't simply the story of Pentheus that has an impact on these wider social myths, it is also how he is embodied, made alive and available to the audience through acting and costume that makes it possible for performance to reinforce or transgress the status quo. We might ask of this image: how do these costumes reinforce or transform attitudes to bodies, identities and social hierarchies in the wider culture? What might spectators feel about their own identities, bodies and social status once the performance has ended? Has the spectator had a sympathetic identification with Pentheus, or Dionysus, or neither, and how has their costuming influenced the possibility of this identification and the possibilities the spectator feels after the performance has ended?

Of course, there is another way in which the costumed figures of Cumming and Curran relate to the wider culture, and that is in the actors' economic and aesthetic relation to the costumes they wear. We might ask whether these actors own the costumes they wear, or whether the theatre owns them. If the theatre does own them, were they specially made for this performance, or drawn from a stock of costumes owned by the company?

How were they paid for: with public funding or private sponsorship, or the profits of the theatre company? These questions concern the process through which costumes are produced in the theatre, but also gesture towards the wider economic system in which actors work, and audiences see performances. If Alan Cumming wears a costume made by Chanel, or a costume sponsored by Phillip Morris Tobacco, its economic status may have a formative effect on how we see the actor. The actor, then, may be seen as a leader of fashion, a servant, a tool of Big Business or a member of an acting fraternity and tradition. Equally, if Curran wears a suit drawn from the theatre stock, that had been used in a previous performance of say, *Waiting for Godot*, the reasons for wearing it might be economic, but the effects may be aesthetic for an audience who see the ghost of Pozzo in the certainties of Pentheus. Costumes have (literally) material qualities, they are an outcome of an economic system in which theatre is made, and their status as commodities, properties or fashion has an aesthetic influence on the meanings of the production.

All of these approaches to watching theatre are useful for a study of costuming. We can look at the relationship between the actor, audience and costume by examining the meanings produced in that relationship, by considering the moments in which the costume appears to escape the illusion, by thinking about the social and theatrical context of the audience, by reflecting on the relation between the images produced by the costuming and the wider status quo and by asking about the economic relations between actor, audience and dress. These are the approaches taken in this book.

Seeing Through Costume

This book suggests that a critical study of costuming can reveal wider insights into the function and effects of the theatre event. Thinking about costuming is a way to think about theatre. Despite this, very few books engage with costume at a critical level. There are some histories of costume that outline what actors wore in the theatre, particularly James Laver's *Costume in the Theatre* (1964), but they have a tendency to treat actors as living paper dolls, rather than fully interrogating the theatrical implications of the *uses* and *reception* of costume. There are also some excellent manuals on making costumes that offer a useful insight into the perspective of the designer, but do not necessarily account for the costumed actor's relation to the audience, such as Tina Bicat's *Making Stage Costumes: A Practical Guide* (2001). There are some excellent cultural and materialist approaches to costume in texts such as Jones and Stallybrass' *Renaissance*

Clothing and the Materials of Memory (2000) and Kaplan and Stowell's *Theatre and Fashion: Oscar Wilde to the Suffragettes* (1995), which offer detailed analyses of costume in the Renaissance and the late nineteenth century respectively, and are very useful for my attempt to offer a broader, less historically based critical approach to costuming. Ann Hollander also offers a helpful history of costume in her book, *Seeing Through Clothes* (1993), which is largely devoted to visual art, and which emphasises ballet, court masques and opera over theatre and dramatic performance.

However, despite the recent explosion of interest in the theories and histories of theatre production, books on scenography by Arnold Aronson (2005), memory by Marvin Carlson (2001), acting by Phillip Zarilli (2002), performance by Philip Auslander (2003); and the materiality of theatre by Rick Knowles (2004) make only passing – if any – reference to costume. These books may note costume's supportive role in creating character, but pay little attention to how costume and make-up might mediate the relationship between the actor and the audience in performance. Theatre scholarship has a tendency to approach the actor as "already dressed", or indeed "already undressed", rather than acknowledging the complex work that costume does in producing the body of the actor under discussion. However, it is possible to suggest that when these scholars consider the actor's body, as many do, they are in fact implicitly discussing costume. Similarly, but inversely, the range of books on cross-dressing by Marjorie Garber (1993), Laurence Senelick (2000), Alisa Solomon (1997) and Lesley Ferris (1993) acknowledge costume's importance, but nonetheless tend to see "through" it to the role it plays in gender formation and representation. Costume, in one way or another, is frequently looked through, around, or over in theatre scholarship.

I want to suggest that a number of implicit, if not explicit, prejudices tend to prevent scholars from engaging directly with the question of costume. First, there is the problem of the anti-visual and text-centred tradition in Western culture that tends to rear its head when it comes to thinking about theatre. Of course, theatre is a highly visual art form, but the traditional philosophical approach has been to repress this dimension of performance, in favour of viewing theatre as simply the manifestation of text onstage (and sometimes, by extension, the greatness of the writer that wrote it). We can see this tendency as far back as Aristotle, who sniffed that

> The Spectacle, though an attraction, is the least artistic of all the parts, and has the least to do with the art of poetry. The tragic effect is quite possible without a public performance and actors; and besides, the getting-up of the Spectacle is more a matter for the costumier than the poet.
>
> (Aristotle, 2001, p. 1462)

As a result of this anti-visual, pro-text tradition, audiences and scholars are often trained to look beyond the surface of the visual landscape of the performance towards the meanings lying *beneath* that landscape. In this approach to theatre, the audience are made to feel that they should ignore the costumes in themselves, and view them simply as the clothes of the character, or as symbolic of the "deeper" emotional or political landscape of the mise-en-scène. The surfaces of costumes are viewed as a means to an end, rather than as an end in themselves. This view is founded upon the assumption that the illusion is of the utmost importance for the experience of a performance, a perspective expressed by the actor and director Samuel West, when he argues that 'the costume should be clothing rather than costume' (Monks, 2008, p. 1). Awareness of costumes *as* costumes is considered a potential threat to the sanctity of the illusion. Instead, costumes are expected to somehow appear to disappear, so that they don't interrupt the flow of the character's presence. Spectators often work very hard to prevent costumes from disrupting their experience at the theatre. This tendency has been repeated in theatre criticism. Despite the interest in the visual dimensions of performance now developing in theatre studies, costumes still tend to be looked past, or through, in analyses of performance.

Of course, connected to this anti-visual tendency is the implicit assumption that costumes are frivolous and not worthy of serious analysis. Perhaps it's no co-incidence that second-hand clothes were called "frippery" in the Renaissance (see Jones and Stallybrass, 2000). Writers may implicitly consider costumes to be a form of frippery, to be far too trivial or playful for serious scholarship. The relationship between stage costume and the wider fashion system is often repressed in discussions of theatre, perhaps through the fear that theatre might seem too bourgeois (an accusation often levelled at it by performance artists and philosophers). By extension, it may be that fashion's associations with femininity (a relatively recent association) may make costumes seem like "girl's stuff": not worthy of serious masculine analysis. However, if we take the work of fashion theorists seriously, who point to the ways in which clothing anchors and produces the social body, and embeds that body within a web of social and economic relations, we might need to acknowledge theatre costume's crucial role in the production of the body onstage. We might also want to turn our attention to the seemingly trivial aspects of costume, the visual playfulness they may introduce to the scene, the enjoyment they may create by revealing cleavages or biceps or ankles and their contribution to the pleasures of spectacle. Thinking of these pleasures is a way to think about what it means to be an audience member at the theatre.

However, I think the most pronounced reason for the widespread absence of critical approaches to costume, has been the problem I raised earlier in the chapter: the essential perceptual indistinguishability between the actor and their costume. When a costumed actor appears onstage, it is often very difficult to tell where the costume leaves off and the actor begins. When we speak of costume, we are often actually talking about actors; and when we speak of actors, we are often actually talking about costume. The fact that it's hard to tell the difference between the actor and their dress makes thinking about costume a difficult task. As a result, this book offers a definition of costume that is inherently paradoxical. Costume is that which is perceptually indistinct from the actor's body, and yet something that can be removed. Costume is a body that can be taken off.

In order to consider the rich possibilities of the costumed actor at the theatre then, it's important to resist the temptation to *interpret*, to look for the meanings beyond or beneath the dress, while ignoring the dress *as* dress. On the other hand, it's also crucial to resist the desire to look at the surfaces alone, to fetishise the object of costume without attending to its possible effects on actor and spectator alike. It is not so much that costume is *only* surface, nor that is it composed of layers of meaning to be unpeeled – like an onion – with a kernel of 'truth' at the centre. Instead, we might imagine viewing costume like a kaleidoscope, with the same ingredients creating new effects and outcomes depending on how it is viewed. When we watch a performance, the meanings and functions of costume might move from being a pleasurable spectacle to becoming an element of set design, or a stage prop. Costume might become indicative of character, inextricable from our engagement with the illusion onstage. Occasionally, however, we might also draw back from this illusion, and wonder how it feels for the actor to wear those clothes, or to wonder what the actor looks like without them. Costume does not remain stable or fully knowable, but rather depends on what we see and how we look at what we see. By studying costume and make-up we can understand what "dressing-up" can do to actors and audiences at the theatre.

Walking Around the Book

Rather than offering a definitive account of costuming's effects, this book proposes a variety of approaches to the costumed actor. Even while the audience may be trained to repress the visibility of costume onstage (although as we'll see in Chapter 2, this has not always been the case), this book looks at some key moments in which costume comes to the forefront of the audience's experience of the actor onstage. These are the moments in which the strangeness of costume and acting become visible. In Chapter 1, I look at how actors' dressing rooms have been represented in novels, paintings and artistic manifestoes, and I draw on the peculiarities of this space to consider the role of costume in the production of the actor's body. In Chapter 2, I argue that costume becomes central to the theatrical experience historically in the moments when the actor is instrumental to the fashion system. Chapter 3 examines Modernist and avant-garde theatre, where artists attempted to make costume realer than the actor onstage. In Chapter 4, I look at how cross-dressing relies on the awareness of the distinction between actors and their costumes, with repercussions for the identity of the performer. In Chapter 5, I think about the actor undressing – a moment when audiences are often acutely aware of costume – and ask whether nudity might be considered a form of dress. In Chapter 6, I look at costumes without bodies through the problem of what ghosts should wear onstage. Finally, in the epilogue, I consider costume as an after-effect of performance in the archive and the museum.

This is a book about actors in costume, but it is imagined from the point of view of the audience at the theatre. There is an important book to be written about the actor's emotional and aesthetic relationship to costume, but this is not it. Instead, I try to imagine what the costumed actor might do to – or for – the spectator at the theatre. Of course, it isn't possible to know exactly what the actor "does" for spectators, so my discussion of audience is not particularly objective. Instead, each chapter opens with a different account of a fictional audience member at the theatre, drawn from novels, films, paintings, short stories, diaries and reviews. These imaginary spectators are variously appalled, perplexed, discombobulated or amused by what they see at the theatre, and costume and the actor are central to their experience. These audience members help me to think through the peculiarities and pleasures of costume at the theatre.

Throughout this book, I will suggest that costuming is indistinguishable from the actor, indeed, that it makes the actor's body possible, and is fundamental to the relationship between the actor and the audience. However, the bodies produced by costuming are not stable objects that are simply "there" on the stage. Rather, these are bodies that are unstable, unreliable and occasionally disconcerting. Costuming might be an act of embodiment, but that embodiment may be partial, fragmented and, as in the case of Pentheus, may lead to dismemberment: to reconfigured and sometimes traumatic bodies on the stage. The multiple, contradictory and uncanny bodies that costuming creates are at the heart of this book.

1

Dressing Rooms: The Actor's Body and Costume

In Emile Zola's 1880 novel *Nana*, Count Muffat visits the actress and prostitute Nana backstage in her dressing room at a Parisian theatre while a show
is in progress. Like Pentheus in the last chapter, Muffat is a morally rigid
man, and he feels overwhelmed by the strangeness of the world of the dressing room: 'Muffat had never been backstage in a theatre and was feeling
particularly surprised and uneasy, full of vague repugnance, not unmixed
with fear' (Zola, 1992, p. 120). And, like Pentheus' double vision after
dressing as a woman, Muffat's repugnance grows into disorientation, due
to the strangely erotic experience of being in close proximity to actors, who
are hard at work dressing up into their costumes:

> Once again, he was feeling overcome by the dizziness [. . .] He could feel the thick
> dressing-room carpet giving way under his feet, and the flames of the gas-jets on
> the dressing table and by the cheval-glass were making a hissing noise around
> his temples. For a second he was scared that this time these women's smells,
> aggravated by the heat, would make him faint.
>
> (Zola, 1992, p. 123)

The disorientation the Count feels is put down to the squalor of the dressing
rooms, and his infatuation with Nana. But I wonder if this light-headedness
is also due to the confusion he feels about being in a third space between
the stage and the real world, a space with a life of its own: its own hierarchy, etiquette, smell and sense of time and space? The Count is confused by
the stark contrast between the painted brilliance of the auditorium and the
'sordid, poverty-stricken garret' (Zola, 1992, p. 140) backstage, and by the
tension between the beauty and skill of the performers on the stage, and the
'pallor and ugliness of actors without their greasepaint' (Zola, 1992, p. 142).
The beauty that had seemed so real to him in performance, is revealed to be

13

nothing but artifice, and he is disconcerted by its loss. But, perhaps Muffat is disoriented most of all by his expectation that the dressing rooms will reveal to him what actors are really like. His hopes are confounded: the work that he sees the actors doing, their act of dressing in preparation for their performance onstage, does not tally with what he sees on the stage or in the street, and he is overwhelmed with dizziness. The dressing room turns out to be an indeterminate place of transition, a place of change, rather than offering any insight into the seams between the illusion and reality.

We might ask why Muffat and Pentheus feel so disoriented by the act of dressing-up: why dressing-up makes the actor and the spectator see double. Muffat and Pentheus's double-seeing suggests that dressing-up transforms the actor's body and psyche, and that it does something peculiar to audiences as well. Imagining actors changing into their costumes then, helps us to consider the process of transformation that costumes might produce, and makes visible the strange permeability between actors' bodies and their clothes. The troubling and disorienting properties of dressing-up begs the question: when we look at an actor in costume onstage, what might we see? Indeed, our theatrical double vision prompts a further question: *how many* actors and *how many* costumes do we see in a single figure? Furthermore, given Muffat's faintness, we could also ask: what forms of double vision are employed by spectators, when looking at the costumed actor? We can think about these questions by making our own visit to the dressing room to consider the strangeness of what we find there. We can also attempt to sketch out the many bodies that costumes produce, and furthermore consider a particular example of how costume has constructed the actor's body (in this case, the body of the actress Fiona Shaw). All of these approaches will allow us to consider the very strange prospect of the actor in costume.

Dressing-Room Bodies

There is a long history of paintings and photographs of performers in their dressing rooms. It is the disorienting qualities of this third space, between the stage and life, that are central to the allure of these pictures. They undertake the task of displaying the seams between the illusion and reality, of showing us what the actor is "really" like offstage. These portraits seem to answer the plaintive cry: 'but what do actors *do*?' It doesn't seem right somehow, that acting is just a job; surely, it must be more mysterious than work, must involve some kind of magic trick of transformation and

Figure 2   Sir Michael Gambon as Sir John Falstaff at the National Theatre 2005 (Stuart Pearson Wright, oil on linen, 2005, by permission of Stuart Pearson Wright).

transportation that might explain what we see onstage? Depictions of this space present different versions of what actors "do", versions of the actor that we can locate in two particular paintings of dressing rooms.

In Stuart Pearson Wright's 2005 portrait of Michael Gambon as Falstaff, *Sir Michael Gambon as Sir John Falstaff at the National Theatre*, Gambon, a well-known actor of the British stage and screen, sits in his dressing room (see Figure 2). His gaze is averted and his stare is one of introspection or reverie. In the mirror on his right, we see his reflection and on the counter we can see a full ashtray and some scripts. The room is corporate looking and bare. It is unclear if Gambon is in costume, or if he's about to get dressed. In another portrait, Degas' 1879 painting *Actress in Her Dressing-room*, we see an unknown performer with her back to us, adjusting her dress (see Figure 3). We can only see her face in the reflection of the mirror. There is a man on her left, helping her with her costume, looking at her body lasciviously. She is entirely focused on her task, and is unaware of our gaze.

Figure 3   Actress in Her Dressing-Room (Edgar Degas, oil on canvas, c. 1879, by permission of The Norton Simon Foundation).

In anonymous portraits, like the Degas, where we know nothing of who the actress really is, we see performers lost in their rapt attention to the act of dressing-up. Our sense of who they are is determined entirely by their relation to costume. By contrast, in pictures of stars, like this one of Michael Gambon, we see the actor already dressed, or about to dress, but in repose, and in this repose we see the idea of the actor as a "man". Here, the picture constructs the idea that the actor is a person with an interior life that is distinct from that of the character's. In the anonymous picture, we see the performer *at work* – and the actor's work as the wearing of costume – while in the image of the star, we see the actor *before or after work*, about to dress up into someone else. Either way, imagining performers putting on (or taking off) their costumes stands in for the secret world behind the illusion of the performance. Access to the dressing room implies that we might somehow discover the seams between actors and their roles. It's no accident that mirrors are often a central feature of these pictures: they stand in for our desire to see behind the theatrical mask, and suggest that actors too might also be searching for their true selves beneath the greasepaint and tulle.

Portraits of actors in dressing rooms reveal some of the cultural suppositions about the relationship between acting and costume. A common feature of many of these pictures is the actor's averted gaze. This averted gaze was a central feature of the recent photographic exhibition at the National Theatre in London in 2007, 'The Half: Photographs of Actors Preparing for the Stage', by the photographer Simon Annand. It is also at the heart of the portrait of Gambon, his averted gaze giving the sense that he is "not performing", but is at a distance from his usual connection with the viewer. The gaze suggests that what we see in Gambon is a kind of reverie that comes before change. His stare implies that acting is an inward activity, a psychic transition from the outside world to the illusion of the stage, and that dressing-up is a crucial linchpin for this shift. The painting of Gambon imagines that dressing-up does something to his psyche, suggesting that changes to the exterior of the body have interior effects, that the surface has repercussions for the soul, and that dressing rooms are places of transition from one psychological state to another. The dressing room, this picture wants to tell us, is a place of interior as well as exterior transformation: it is quite literally a changing room.

However, while locating the distinction between actors and their roles is a major trope of dressing-room pictures, there is another important dimension to these paintings, which is the slightly sordid pleasure of peeking backstage unnoticed. In the Degas painting, for instance, we can look at the actress without fear of being confronted. Her absorption in the adjustment of her costume positions us as voyeurs, free to look at her body without her knowledge. Perhaps the man in the painting on her left is our surrogate in this desire to look? The appeal is erotic, but it also hinges on this idea that the painting reveals the secret world of the performer, whose central ingredient is the mundane. Crucially, the actress isn't doing anything very interesting: her adjustments to her dress point to the repetitive work of performance. Indeed, even as the Gambon portrait might suggest a spiritual dimension to the actor's identity, accounts of dressing rooms often focus on the mediocrity of the actor's activities there. What we see in these paintings (and find in representations of dressing rooms in novels, diaries, plays and poems) is the everyday routine labour of being an actor: the graft and repetition that exist beneath the seemingly spontaneous spectacle. The secret of the actor's work is that there is none: it turns out that the "magic" of the stage is conjured up through dull and hard work. This mundanity is crucial to the allure of the dressing room, and is often used as a metaphor for the work of the actor. The erotic act of looking at an actor dressing-up is tempered – or perhaps heightened – by the fact that dressing-up is an every-day activity that appears dislocated from the fantastical stage-world that the performer inhabits for the audience.

On the other hand, the dressing room can also establish the star persona of the actor. Dressing-up can be an act that asserts the hierarchies of the backstage world. Zola's description of the communal dressing rooms shared by the minor actors in *Nana* emphasises the mundane labour of dressing and undressing backstage: 'the final scramble was taking place, everybody cleaning off all the roughened grease-paint, pulling on their clothes, in a cloud of rice-powder' (Zola, 1992, p. 138). By contrast, Jennifer Lopez's demand 'that her Top of the Pops dressing-room be painted completely white and filled with fresh white flowers' (Gannon, 2007, p. 24) is situated in a long line of dressing-room demands that have ensured that the identity of the performer as a star is foremost. Muffat's double vision back-stage might be explained, therefore, by the ways that the location and décor of the dressing room, and the sorts of activities that go on there (dressing or thinking) do crucial work in deciding what sort of actor we see onstage. The relations of space, objects, hierarchy and activity in the dressing room show us what a complex and fragile figure the actor is, and how the location where actors get dressed and undressed can exert a formative effect on their public personae.

Of course, the twentieth century was a time when the relationship between dressing-up and the theatrical hierarchy was challenged. Included in Vsevlod Meyerhold's revolutionary approach to theatre in Russia in the 1920s, was a reconsideration of the role and meaning of dressing rooms, asking:

> What link should there be between the actor and the place where he is about to perform? Should he sit in his dressing room, remote from the acting area, and simply arrive in time to speak his part on cue? Or is it better to place him in close proximity to the stage, so that he can easily, naturally, organically merge into the performance at the appropriate moment?
>
> (Meyerhold, 1972, p. 70)

Meyerhold's (rhetorical) questions imply that to revolutionise perfor-mance practices onstage, it is necessary to reconfigure the hierarchies offstage, including those inscribed in the act of dressing-up. Similarly, Ari-ane Mnouchkine's company, the Théâtre du Soleil in Paris, make their dressing rooms visible to the audience (see Miller, 2007, p. 90). Again, Mnouchkine's impulse is to reconfigure the audience/actor relationship. In theory, when actors dress up in full view, the audience are more likely to relate to them as working actors than as characters. The gap between the actor and the role that the Degas and Gambon portraits seek to locate in the dressing room is a gap that has been placed centre stage in the twentieth century by directors such as Meyerhold, Mnouchkine and Bertolt Brecht. It could be argued however, that systematising the act of dressing-up renders the actor's working body part of the stage's illusion, becoming another fictional role. Dressing-up onstage offers no further insight into the secrets of the actor's work.

The Actor's Body

While we cannot really tell the difference between these performers and their clothes (and in Gambon's case we are unsure if his clothes are costume or not), these paintings and photographs express the desire to try to locate the difference, to try to establish a distinction between actors and their costumes. In all cases, the attempt fails. We cannot distinguish between the performers and what they wear: their clothes constitute their selves in the paintings. After all, when we look at the portrait of Michael Gambon, it's not entirely clear whom we see. The real man, Gambon, and the illusion, Falstaff, are not easily distinguished: it's not clear if we are looking at Gambon in costume. But, even if it were clear that Gambon was dressed for his role, we are not necessarily seeing Gambon *as* Falstaff. Instead, it's as if there is a third Michael Gambon, the dressing-room Gambon, who occupies this peculiar space between stage and life. While actors put on the clothes of their character in the dressing room, they may only partly do so, they might wait until the last minute before finishing putting on their costume, they may have only half their make-up done. Within this strange space of dressing-up, the costume is not the character's clothes, and not the man's, but is the actor's work clothes: the uniform, or overalls that they do their job in.

We can see then, in pictures of actors dressing-up, a range of possible figures at work: the star actor, the real actor, the working actor and the transforming actor. These figures can also be found on the stage, operating alongside and within the character in the fictional narrative. When spectators look at a costumed actor on the stage, they see many actors and many costumes. These figures often exist only at the corner of the eye when watching a performance, but are nonetheless essential to how the character may be received by the audience. Sometimes the form of performance indicates that the audience should not look at these figures too directly, while in other forms, like in the work of Mnouchkine and Brecht, or in ballet, circus or celebrity West End appearances, they become central to the spectator's experience of the performance. The multiple figures in operation in performance are configured in varying relationships of prominence and visibility depending on the contexts, aesthetics and traditions informing the style of acting, and the viewing attitudes of the audience. Portraits of actors in their dressing rooms may function to allow spectators to contemplate the often repressed aspects of the actor's work, freezing the motion of these many bodies.

So, when spectators look at an actor in this semi-dressed state, or indeed, when they look at an actor in costume on the stage, whom and what do they see? The borders between the actor and the costume are unclear. The costume is the spectator's means to access the actor's body, and is also a means for the actor to access the world of the performance. When spectators watch an actor in performance they might imagine they see only one figure, but if they were to relax their eyes slightly, this single figure would blur into multiple ones, all of whom are doing a different job in performance, all of whom are a product of the performance. These blurred and multiple figures might even suggest that the actor's body is a composite of many bodies. Using the word "body" suggests that we need to approach the actor not as a given, real object, but as a process: a series of practices that are ongoing. When spectators look at actors in costume, they see bodies emerging continuously through the course of the performance. A view of the body as a process may be counterintuitive in a post-Darwinian world, where the body is often assumed to be an object beyond culture, determined only by hereditary and genetic forces. But, even if we accept this version of the body (and many people don't), we can still take account of the social frameworks through which we approach, or imagine, or experience the body (our own and other people's). In other words, we can't leave our context behind when we look at bodies, and actors can't leave their context behind when playing them. If we work with this notion of a body as a process, we can imagine actors emerging in various forms on the stage, depending on their historical context and aesthetic function within the theatrical event. So far, I have labelled the various figures of the actor as working, real, star and transforming, but I want to suggest that we can break the actor's body down into even more specific categories. We can examine these bodies more closely in order to understand the complex set of relationships between actors and their costumes. These approaches to the actor have been discussed in detail by Bert States (1985), Michael Quinn (1990) and David Graver (2003), and I'm drawing on their ideas in the following discussion.

We have already seen evidence of the "working body" in the Degas portrait of the actress, in her intent focus on the labour of dressing. This body also emerges on the stage, and as Bert States points out, we can find evidence of its existence in the sweat produced on the brow of the actor while they perform the role (States, 2003, p. 109). This sweat is the working body's sweat, not the character's (although sometimes they coincide, as when Falstaff sweats from overeating, and the working figure of Gambon simultaneously sweats from the heat of the lights). Costume makes the working body possible, in facilitating its unnatural state, its: 'corporeal elasticity and expertise' (Graver, 2003, p. 160), establishing its particular and peculiar relationship with the stage environment. After all, some costumes are designed to foreground the performers' work, such as the unitard of the strongman at the circus, while other costumes actually constitute the work, such as clown stilts or the magically transforming costumes of the Kabuki stage. Even modern-dress productions of Shakespeare determine the attitude of the actor's body onstage, establishing the freedoms and constrictions and contours of a body that appears very like the spectator's. The appearance, abilities and dimensions of the working body are produced and rendered meaningful through costume.

The "aesthetic body" is made of codes and conventions. Gambon's costume might look like ordinary dress, but his beige trousers or white pointed shoes and red stripy socks (if indeed they are costume) enter into symbolic realm once included in the space of the stage. His white shoes and socks might become significant of a certain form of dandyism, if every other actor wears sensible brown shoes, for example. His beige trousers would become immediately symbolic if the other actors were dressed in army uniforms. The aesthetic body is therefore a body that is defined by a history of codes, and costumes are permeated by this history: a fan for a restoration play, or an Elizabethan cod-piece for example, presume a set of preordained performance styles, which may have no correlation with actual historical practices, but occupy their own theatrical lineage. After all, clothes that are rarely seen in everyday life can be utterly familiar in stage performance. A black hat, cloak and pronounced facial hair might communicate villainy on the stage, and look odd anywhere else. The audience's previous experiences of theatre will enable them to recognise and interpret clothing that they may have never seen beyond stage or screen performance.

Furthermore, the aesthetic body can function as part of the design of a production, communicating atmosphere, creating spectacle and sometimes working as a substitute for the set. Indeed, costume is one of the main ways in which directors and designers can depict a historical period on the stage. The use of historical costuming is frequently one of the main expressions of a director's interpretation of a play text, becoming significant of the context of the narrative, and the vision of the director. Aesthetic costuming can also work to render actors scenic objects, a tendency particularly true of the early twentieth-century theatre, where Edward Gordon Craig's vision of the actor as an "Uber-Marionette" (a concept discussed at length in Chapter 3) resulted in costumes that were more directly connected to set design, than to the expression of character. In this way, the aesthetic body often functions as a surrogate for the designer or director's body, and costume is codified in order to become consistent with the overall approach to the stage setting.

The "self-expressive body" is the body whose persona competes with that of the character's and is often established through virtuoso acting, or celebrity performance (see States, 1985, p. 160). Self-expressive bodies draw the spectator's attention to the presence of the actors' "real" selves alongside the characters they are playing. This effect may have taken place in Gambon's performance, if a particular mannerism or pattern of speech reminded a spectator of his previous role in "that thing on the TV". In this moment, the figure of Gambon emerges, seemingly in his own right, out-performing the figure of Falstaff. Michael Quinn points out that this is a particularly common effect of celebrity actors onstage, who (often inadvertently) interrupt the illusion of the character in favour of their own presence (Quinn, 1990, p. 155). However, as Quinn shows, the "real" self of the actor is also a fiction; a composite of qualities based on the roles the actor has played previously, the gossip and publicity about the actor's private life, the reviews of their work, etc. The actor's "real" self, therefore, is a performance alongside the performance of the illusion, an exterior referent, which is itself a product of the performance. While the "real" Gambon may appear to interrupt the illusion of Falstaff, this interruption comes in the form of another fictional character.

Costume's support for this self-expressive tendency is historically variable, and in the next chapter we will see how the self-expressive body may be prioritised or repressed in various historical moments. Costume may make star actors familiar, by dressing them in clothes that are reminiscent of their previous roles, or may make them look radically different to how they are usually perceived. However, looking completely different may be received by the audience as a testament to the actor's great skill, and may thereby shore up the actor's star status (a tendency seen recently in the desire of beautiful Hollywood actresses to appear ugly on film). Or, costume may work to highlight the difficulty of the task of the performer, foregrounding glimpses of bulging muscles or a sweat-covered brow, signalling to us that the task the actor has undertaken is mammoth and worthy of praise. Equally, costume may actually constitute the self-expressive tendency, as on the eighteenth-century stage, where innovations in costume were attributed to the actor's prowess in interpreting their role. The actor

David Garrick placed a horse-hair wig on top of his ordinary wig to play Macbeth, for example (see Laver, 1964, p. 100), an innovation which was heralded as sign of the actor's greatness (we will see more of Garrick's way with wigs in Chapter 6). Costume that foregrounds the self-expressive body often functions as decoration, and inevitably extends to the display of the actor's body itself as a source of visual pleasure, framing, emphasising and revealing it in ways that we can admire. Self-expressive costume competes with that of the character's for prominence on the stage.

The "character's body" is central to the fabric of the illusion woven on the stage. Like the aesthetic body, the character's costume is situated within a history of conventions. The costuming tradition that Hamlet should look thin, or that Vladimir and Estragon should be dressed as tramps in Beckett's *Waiting for Godot*, are based on scant textual sources and a rich theatrical history, which mould and mediate the character's body. Illusion has internal codes and histories of its own, and the character's body has a peculiar relationship with the "real" as a result. If theatre prioritises this body, focusing more on maintaining the illusion than on giving way to the expressive, aesthetic or working bodies of the actor, costume is expected to appear to disappear, to become so fused with the reality of the character that it appears an inevitability. In the character mode, Gambon's costume should ideally reappear as Falstaff's clothes. In this way, costume "sinks" into the character, as Bert States suggests: 'the purely gratuitous mixture [...] becomes inevitable, a synthesis expressive of something ideal, irresistible' (States, 1985, p. 121). However, costume appearing as dress does not automatically have anything to do with realism – which is no realer than any other style of performance – but relies instead on the internal coherence of the performance style, and on an audience trained to prioritise the referential body over other modes. According to States: 'the "suspension of disbelief" [...] depends only on the power of the image to serve as a channel for what of reality is of immediate interest to the audience' (States, 2003, p. 131).

The "sensate body" describes the sensations undergone by the performer onstage while wearing costume. Sensation is one of the most private experiences for the actor, and can never be absolutely known by the audience. As David Graver suggests, 'the performers stand between two worlds: the one in the spectator's eyes and the one inside their own bodies' (Graver, 2003, p. 173). Of course, there is a third body in this, the sensate body that the audience imagines the actor experiencing. When watching an actor trapped in a mound for two hours, like the actress playing Winnie in Beckett's *Happy Days*, or indeed when watching one desirable actor kiss another, the audience may imagine their visceral experience through projected sensation. This effect also applies to the audience's relation to the actor's costume. The transformation of the actor's body has potential effects on the spectator's. Clothing produces an empathic response – part of the experience of watching performance comes from imagining how it might feel to dress as a gorilla, or to wear high heels (sometimes all at once).

This visceral empathy can be used to serve our identification with the character. An actress playing Hedda Gabler, for example, might use the constriction of her corset to communicate Hedda's sense of entrapment (as Fiona Shaw did in the production I discuss later in this chapter). This use of costume relies on the audience imagining wearing a corset – not being able to breathe properly, and the feeling of constriction – in order to grasp at the experience of the actor *and* the character on the stage. The spectator's relationship with the actor in performance is often mediated by the feelings created by wearing clothes. This experience, it seems to me, is particularly prominent when watching classical ballet, where the self-expressive body and the sensate body battle for prominence. On the one hand, the virtuosity of the dancers conceals the pain involved in dancing in pointe shoes, on the other hand, the pain that the dancers *might* be feeling, or rather the sensations that audience members think *they* would feel if *they* danced on *their* toes, interrupts the flow of the virtuosity. At least for my part, the experience of watching ballet vacillates from the transportation of virtuosity, to a form of phenomenological wincing.

The "historical body" is the product of the social belief systems circulating around the body. However, the historical body may not resemble a body on the street, but is rather representative of the fantasies and contradictions surrounding the body in the wider culture. Costume is central to the construction of the historical body on the stage, an effect that can be seen in the blackened cork faces of the minstrel stage, the ragged clothes of the stage Irishman, or the exaggerated femininity of the pantomime dame (we will examine these bodies more closely in Chapter 4). At first glance, Gambon does not seem to be representative of any particular version of the historical body. However, the painting's suggestion that he is *thinking* imagines a particular vision of the body that is somehow distinct from the self. Gambon's self is not located in his feet or his long hands, but rather found in his gaze, suggesting that his sense of self is on the inside rather than on the outside of the body. Of course, "inside" and "outside" are metaphors, rather than accurate descriptions, but they are very powerful metaphors that have a history. The self has not always been imagined as inside, or distinct from, the body: the medieval period, for example, imagined the self as located in clothes. The idea that thinking is something that happens beyond or within the body is the product of a series of philosophical and historical shifts that inform the composition of this painting, and how it might be read. Similarly, audiences will frame their engagement with the actor's body through a series of historically determined assumptions about what the body is, what it looks like, how it behaves and what it means. These assumptions also inform how actors embody characters, and how acting itself is imagined.

To return now to the actor in the dressing room, we find that we see not a single body or a single costume, but many costumes that produce many bodies. The costumed actor, therefore, is a composite of different theatrical practices, or modes, that come in and out of focus. Indeed, sometimes it's the tensions between these bodies that produce the meanings of the performance. Costume works as a hinge in the audience's vacillation between the different versions of the actor's body, although of course, these bodies aren't completely distinct and they don't come into focus in orderly succession. Instead, these bodies emerge in and through each other through the messy process that is the experience of watching a show. How might we see this process in action? We could approach this issue by examining an actor in a specific production, in order to consider how these bodies come in and out of focus. We might consider a performance of a specific character through time, in order to catalogue the variable relations between these different bodies. But we might also focus on a single actor in a series of roles and consider how spectators have viewed the actor's body. Of course, we can't ever really know how spectators view an actor, but we can examine the opinions of that deeply problematic version of the spectator: the critic. Critics may not tell us much about what an audience "really thought" about a production, but their reviews often reveal a lot about the wider set of values around the historical body, and its relation to the character's body. They may also reveal the orthodoxies of how the various bodies of the actor are expected to balance and emerge. A study of the reception of a single actor in a variety of roles in reviews and interviews helps to elucidate how the actor's body accumulates its own history of meanings through its costuming. We can consider the particular case of the actor Fiona Shaw whose body has been continually reformulated through costuming, and through the reception of that costuming in a variety of roles.

Dressing Fiona Shaw

Fiona Shaw is an Irish-born actress who has been known for her work on the British classical stage, and her occasional appearance in film roles (such as *Harry Potter*) since the 1980s. Her work has been particularly characterised by her virtuoso approach to well-known classical roles in plays by writers such as Shakespeare, Ibsen, Brecht, Beckett and Euripides. In the reception of her work, her bodies are framed in three key ways by reviewers: (1) in how she describes her work in interview, (2) in the reviews of her performances and (3) in the accumulation of her roles, which have had an intertextual effect on how her body is viewed. Throughout her career, critics have commented upon Shaw's sometimes controversial approach to her costumes onstage. These costumes have not only been considered for their depiction of character, but have also been viewed as expressions or depictions of Shaw's identity and theatrical status, which can be seen in how she and her long-time collaborator, the director Deborah Warner, have been framed in terms of gender identity in the reviews and interviews on their work. Commentary on Shaw and her costumes tends to be characterised by slippages between her fictional roles, her personality, her virtuosity and her gender, all of which combine to figure and reconfigure her body in performance.

In reviews and interviews, critics frequently equate Shaw's virtuosity onstage with her intellect off it, suggesting that: 'interviewing Shaw is like having the top of your head taken off and your cranium scoured out with a brillo pad' (Rutter, 1997, p. 314). The slippage between Shaw's theatrical intelligence and personal intelligence is continued in the descriptive connections made between her character traits and her body. The following description is typical: 'Shaw's talent is prodigious, her onstage presence imposing: rail-thin with close-cropped hair, she is angular and intense, exuding sharpness, exactitude, precision' (Coen, 1997, p. 12). And another interviewer finds proof of Shaw's temperament in her physiognomy: 'She has an undeniable imperiousness. This extends even to her bone structure' (French, 1991, p. 7). The critical recognition of Shaw's strength as a performer configures the description of her body, where even her bone structure reflects her personal qualities. The sharpness of her mind leads to the sharpness of her limbs and the imperiousness of her nose results, Pinocchio-like, from her classical roles on the stage. Reviewers and interviewers suggest that it is difficult, if not impossible, to distinguish between how Shaw acts and how she looks: her body is moulded by the reception of her performances.

The slippage between the descriptions of Shaw's acting style and her physique extends to her gender identity. Reviewers imbue her body with the characteristics they attach to her status as a powerful, successful woman, suggesting that she has 'a drive and intensity common among professional women who live alone, rejecting the comforts and confinements of domesticity in order to dedicate themselves to their work' (Brown, 1995, p. 25). And she and Warner are frequently compared in terms of gender and physique: 'they look similar in type: tall, lean, purposeful, single women in their thirties, striding one would suppose towards their prime' (Peter, 1991, p. 10). Shaw's status and physique not only signal power, but also self-denial. Her thinness is interpreted as the rejection of domesticity, her height is a sign of ambition, and she and Warner are described as "striding" rather than "strolling", or "ambling", through their careers, as if their movement through space was a symptom of their single status. Even while Shaw is applauded for her success and skill, that success also signals a lack or denial, which marks the appearance of her body.

Notably, British critics frequently compare Shaw with other famous star actors: Vanessa Redgrave, Sara Bernhardt and even Laurence Olivier (see French, 1991, p. 7). Shaw's body is situated within an accumulated history of other actor's performances, imbuing her with their authority and power. Her virtuosity as an actor places her within the legacies of other actors and other roles, positioning her body within a genealogy of classical performance. Shaw is established as a star in reviews, therefore, by positioning her within a tradition of star performance, reconfiguring how we might see her body through the memory of other actors. This status within the classical hierarchy is supported by Shaw's emphasis in interview on the qualities of hard work, rigor, mastery and risk, when describing her work. She puts her success down to her work ethic: 'I suppose doing well means working very hard [. . .] and I work very hard' (McFerran, 1994, p. 31). Shaw's description of her work frames her performances as virtuoso, as Bert O. States suggests: 'virtuosity, in theater as in athletics is not simply skill, but skill displayed against [the] odds' (States, 1985, p. 162). Shaw's virtuosity positions her as the originator of meaning in relation to her work onstage and situates her within the history of other virtuoso performers on the British stage.

These discursive slippages: from the roles Shaw performs; to her virtuosity; to the kind of person she is; to sort of actor she is like; and finally to the kind of woman she is; cumulatively reconstruct her body anew. As Michael Quinn argues, even while the spectator may feel they can access the "real" actor as distinct from the character onstage, the figure of the real actor is just as theatrical as the fictional character they play (see Quinn, 1990, p. 155). It is notable that this construction of Shaw's body goes on to inform and interrogate the characters she plays onstage. The interrelationship between the real Shaw and her fictional characters produces a series of fascinating bodies onstage, bodies which are produced through the relationship between Shaw's approach to costume and the critics' attitudes to her body in performance.

The formative relationship between costume and the body of the actor could be seen in Warner and Shaw's first collaboration, Sophocles' *Electra*, which took place at the Royal Shakespeare Theatre in 1988. The play centres on the character of Electra who is in mourning for her dead father whom her mother Clytemnestra (and her mother's lover) has murdered. Electra is rendered inactive and ineffective in her grief, her longing for her exiled brother and her hatred for her mother. In Warner's production, Shaw emerged from behind an enormous metal door, naked under a ripped black tunic, which exposed her legs, the side of her torso, her arms and occasionally her breasts. The blackness of the costume emphasised the pallor of her body and also created an aesthetic connection with the chorus, who were swathed in long black robes and scarves, which covered their heads and faces. The concealment of the chorus' bodies acted as a stark contrast to the exposure of Shaw's, and established a convention of the "normal" concealed bodies of the chorus in comparison to the "abnormally" exposed body of Shaw. Shaw, grazed and bruised, emaciated, and with her head partly shaven, performed Electra as a character literally doubled over with grief.

While female nudity often operates as a site of desire for an audience, the costume's exposure of Shaw's flesh had the opposite effect, and produced a disturbing and transgressive portrait of femininity on the stage. The critics' responded to Shaw's performance by seeing her Electra as asexual, ungendered and androgynous. Irving Wardle in *The Times* described Shaw's Electra as 'a ragged, half naked spectre whose very gender is obliterated by grief' (Wardle, 1988, p. 27). Jane Edwardes in *Time Out* added: 'her body naked under a black shift, she presents an uninhibited portrait of a woman – unsexed, unhinged and uncompromising – clawing at her flesh' (Edwardes, 1989, p. 14), and Michael Billington described Shaw's Electra as a 'wild, strange, driven, a somewhat asexual creature' (Billington, 1989, p. 11). The spectacle of Shaw's body semi naked onstage without that nudity expressing conventionally desirable femininity became unreadable *as* femininity to the critics, leading them to view her figure through the blurred category of androgyny. Their response reveals how costume, makeup and gestural codes are central to the construction of femininity on the stage. Shaw's Electra did not dress or behave in a conventionally feminine way, and critics not only considered her unfeminine, but deemed her fundamentally no longer female.

Shaw's costume revealed her body in such a way as to eradicate its femininity. However, even while Shaw played a woman who was physically, politically and emotionally powerless, the power of her performance unsettled Electra's passivity. In *Electra*, Shaw's performance of disempowerment paradoxically established her as the most theatrically powerful figure in the production. Watching Shaw on the stage combined the suffering figure of the character Electra, with the damaged body-in-pain of the working Shaw, and the powerful, skilful and controlling figure of the self-expressive Shaw (see Melrose, 1994). While the audience were presented with the body of a disempowered and disenfranchised character, they were also presented with the figure of a powerful, intelligent and successful actress playing that woman on the stage. The tension between the self-expressive qualities of Shaw's performance and the body of the character unsettled the representation of gender in Sophocles' play and produced a complex portrait of femininity in performance.

A similar tension between the disempowerment of character and the self-expressive power of the actor could be seen in Shaw's performance as Hedda Gabler at the Abbey Theatre, Dublin in 1991 (also directed by Warner). Henrik Ibsen's play centres on Hedda's unhappiness in her marriage, which is partly due to her pregnancy, (which is hinted at but never overtly acknowledged in the text), and her combination of traditionally feminine and masculine traits, which rendered her a subversive figure on the nineteenth-century stage. Hedda's mental imprisonment was displayed through Shaw's physical confinement, in the spatial restrictions created by the furniture on the cluttered stage, and in the rigidity of her corseted costume. Shaw looked uncomfortable in her costume and there was a blurring between the actor's working body struggling with the physical discomforts of the costume, and the symbolic effect of Hedda's entrapment in bourgeois society. This tension was maintained further by the vignette at the beginning of the production, where Shaw/Hedda appeared onstage in a night-time scene, feeling despairingly beneath her nightgown to check for menstrual blood, referencing the play's subtext of Hedda's unwanted pregnancy. Shaw's active presence in the voluminous nightdress established a contrast to the subsequent rigidity imposed by her corset, and the audience were invited to read between the appearance of bourgeois respectability and the internal struggle within Hedda, through Shaw's struggle with her costume. Again, the presence of Shaw functioned variously as the working body of the actor struggling with the demands of the role, the character's body, and the self-expressive body, which emerged as an "author" of the meanings of Hedda onstage. Shaw's costumed body both performed the character and enacted a critique of the historical body that the character was forced to perform.

The relationship between the "real" Fiona Shaw and her fictional role was complicated further by her performance as Richard II in the National Theatre in 1995, again directed by Deborah Warner. Warner and Shaw came to this production having been embroiled in controversy over costume during their performance of Beckett's *Footfalls* in 1995 (see O'Toole, 2008).

Shaw wore a red dress, instead of the grey dress required by the text, and Warner and Shaw were banned for life from directing and performing Beckett by the writer's estate. This controversy surrounding authorial intent and costume followed them into their production of Shakespeare's *Richard II*. Even before the production opened, the newspapers were seething at the controversial prospect of Shaw playing the title role. The objections to the cross-casting of Shaw was summed up by one critic who said: 'much as I believe in the power of great acting to suspend disbelief, there are limits' (Temple, 1995, p. 23). Suddenly, Shaw's self-expressive virtuoso body when playing Electra and Hedda became a historical body: the femaleness of Shaw was viewed as an interruption not only of the character of Richard, but of the reality of monarchy itself. While there has been a long tradition of playing Richard as effeminate by male actors, a *woman* playing the role was considered inappropriate for the portrayal of a king, so that the intensity Shaw brought to Electra was now criticised in her portrait of Richard. Costume was a central mechanism through which Richard's body was invoked onstage by Shaw, and rejected by the critics.

Richard's body was first established by the contrast between Shaw's costume and that of the other actors onstage. The male characters were dressed in naturalistic costumes, which were designed based on portraits of medieval royalty. Shaw, on the other hand, was wrapped in bandages from her chest down to her ankles, producing an aesthetic body that occupied a different theatrical realm to that of the other actors. The bandages could be interpreted as symbolising the ritualised body of the king: they became a way of immortalising Richard's body, and acted as a portent of his death: 'as if Richard's body were already swaddled in a winding sheet' (Rutter, 1997, p. 319–320). Alternatively, the costume could be read as foregrounding Shaw's cross-dressed status, making the bandaging and flattening of her breasts a visible feature of her performance. The fact that the costume drew attention to the act of dressing-up drew a distinction between Shaw and her role, asserting her working body. The fact that the bandages could be read as either symbolic of Richard's divine body, or as foregrounding Shaw's working body, blurred the relationship between the two figures, allowing the costume to operate both on the character and self-expressive levels of performance. The divine body of the king was rendered equivalent to the doubled body of the actor, and theatricality and monarchy were integrally linked within Shaw's costuming.

This theatricality was at the heart of why the critics viewed Shaw's costume so negatively, seeing it as a disruption of the otherwise 'historical" approach of the production. One critic saw her costume as too stylised and modern: 'Shaw's costume is a bit too suggestive of a Comme des

Garcons outfit' (Koenig, 1995, p. 22), while others felt it referred back to Shaw's previously self-immolating performances, seeing in the bandages: 'the nightmarish thought [...] that this is because the actress had been drawing so much blood with the self mutilation that was a harrowing feature of her Electra' (Spencer, 1995, p. 17). Overall, the critics raised concerns that the costume was out of kilter with the other actor's bodies on the stage, and furthermore detracted from the reality of the historical figure of King Richard II. This criticism betrayed the confusion, widespread in the critical commentary on the production, between the fictional figure of Richard in Shakespeare's play, and the "real" Richard of English history. Shaw's abstract and symbolic costuming was viewed as a challenge to the reality of monarchy itself.

The threat posed by Shaw's costume to the representation of the monarchy, could also be located in Shaw's ambivalent gender identity in performance. While critics attacked her ability represent masculinity, with one critic arguing that: 'Shaw doesn't have enough maleness to play Peter Pan' (Koenig, 1995, p. 22), they simultaneously criticised her for being inadequately feminine, with another critic describing her as: 'a lean, angular woman with a sharp jutting jaw [who] is not particularly attractive' (Richard Hornby, 1996, p. 10). In contrast to her positive reviews for portraying women, in which her ambiguity and complexity was praised (although reduced to the category of androgyny), Shaw as Richard was criticised for her inadequate femininity as an actor – and as a woman – and at the same time denounced for being 'a stereotypical girlie' (Koenig, 1995, p. 22). While Shaw was praised for performing critical and deconstructive versions of femininity as Electra and Hedda, her deconstruction of the role of Richard was less acceptable to critics who asserted her "real" body as female, and therefore unable to carry the weight of monarchy and the authority of Shakespearean tragic roles. As Shaw herself said: 'if a man had been doing what I was doing in the part, reviewers would have been thrilled. But a woman playing that sort of thing was more than a little sacrilegious. You can't have a girl playing a king and then acting like being a king isn't serious' (Rutter, 1997, p. 323). However, after the performance of *Richard II* had ended it became evident that Shaw's body had been reconfigured and remoulded by the memory of her performance once more. When an American critic reviewed Warner and Shaw's performance of T. S. Eliot's *The Wasteland* in 1995, he remarked: 'seeing [Shaw] onstage for the first time, I can well imagine her as Richard. I have a little more difficulty visualizing her in female roles' (Simon, 1996, p. 9). Shaw's body was layered with the ghosts of previous roles, which informed the reception of her portrayal of Richard, and remoulded the reception of her body.

Similarly, Shaw's portrayal of Medea in Warner's production at the Abbey Theatre, Dublin in 2000, played on the memory of her performances of Electra and Hedda. Like Electra, Medea has been dispossessed by the desertion of her husband Jason, although unlike Electra, Medea takes control of her fate with terrifying results. Shaw-as-Medea was first heard from below the stage raging at Jason's injustices. However, when she entered the public playing space, her Medea was unexpectedly muted and embarrassed. The contrast between her private wailing self – reminiscent of Shaw's portrayal of Electra – and her public understated persona dressed in a black cocktail dress, matching cardigan and high heeled shoes, resembling an Irish middle-class suburban housewife, created: 'at once the unsettling sense of a woman constructing a public self' (O'Toole, 2000, p. 59). Shaw's performance was consciously theatrical. Tottering slightly in her high heels, Medea was a woman who was *playing* at the role of wife and mother, attempting to conform to the social mores of the culture she had adopted, but who was ill at ease and uncomfortable with the part she was playing. Shaw showed Medea's clothing to *be* a costume, revealing her "foreignness" to the clothing she wore. Shaw's high heels and short dress became a metaphor for the constricting social role that Medea was forced to play in Corinth. Her relationship to her costume made Medea appear a modern-day Hedda, with Shaw's struggle with the confines of the costume reading again as the character's struggle with her social role.

Shaw wore a similar black cocktail dress to play Winnie in Beckett's *Happy Days* at the National Theatre in London in 2007, although this time, she wore it with a straw hat. Having had the ban lifted by the Beckett estate, Warner and Shaw's production was ghosted by their controversies around costume. Would this Winnie, trapped in her mound with only her husband and handbag to distract her, wear a red dress, or indeed a grey dress to match the mound she was sunk in? Instead, it seemed that Medea in her cocktail dress had been caught in rock, perhaps sometime in her flight to Athens, and taken on the mantle of Winnie. The intertextual nature of this costume was foregrounded even further when Warner and Shaw toured *Happy Days* to the ancient theatre of Epidaurus in Greece, possibly one of the places where *Medea* was first performed. It appeared that Medea, in the guise of Winnie, had come home.

Looking for the "real Fiona Shaw" is like looking for the truth in a hall of mirrors: Shaw is continually refracted, distorted and reflected through a variety of incarnations that often exist simultaneously on the stage. Shaw's expressive and working bodies emerge according to the weight of history and memory invested in the characters that she plays, and the spectator's relation to her body is configured and reconfigured accordingly. Contrary to

Erica Fisher Lichte's view that: 'theater proceeds on the basis of the body as an a priori. [...] The actor's body is the condition, as it were, which makes theater possible' (Lichte, 1992, p. 67), an examination of the effects of Fiona Shaw's persona on the meanings of her performances, is a convincing case for the idea that it is *costuming* that makes the actor's body possible. Shaw's working, expressive and character bodies are not independent, but rather mutually inform the meanings and reception of her work. Furthermore, Shaw's appearance has been continually remoulded by her reception in performance, suggesting that when spectators look at the costumed actor, their act of looking has a formative effect on the actor's body, reshaping its contours and reconfiguring its meanings due to the cumulative effects of performance. The actor's body is not singular and stable, but rather multiple and continually shifting in its appearance and possibilities.

Dressing and Disorientation

To return to the shaken and dizzy Count Muffat in Nana's dressing room, we can see that his disorientation may be a response to his recognition that costume is formative: it is not simply reflective of the inner states of characters, or a decoration of the actor's appearance, but is rather constitutive of the actor's inner and outer body. Actors in dressing rooms are incomplete bodies. Muffat is confronted by bodies that reveal their multiplicity in their half-dressed state. The actor's body is, after all, a series of practices rather than a finished object. Actors practice their own bodies by wearing and using costume – and their bodies are also worn and used *by* costumes. The audience gain imaginative access to actors' bodies through their clothes. In the end, there is no difference between actors and their costumes.

This half-finished body is central to the allure of the dressing-room pictures, but it is also the reason for the fact that these portraits always in the end renege on their promise to show us the difference between actors and acting. When it comes to it, these pictures disappoint. Acting remains unknowable: hermetically sealed from prying eyes. The problem that always undermines portraits of actors in their dressing rooms is that once actors are looked at – even if they appear not to notice – their activity turns into fictional labour, they still appear to be *acting* even if their averted gaze and their absorption in the task of dressing suggests otherwise. Dressing-room portraits promise to reveal the mysteries of acting, but they end up perpetuating it further, making the private life of the actor all the more secretive and unknowable. The "real" actor is in the end a fantasy of portraits of dressing-up.

2

Dressing the Audience:
A History of Fashion
at the Theatre

At the heart of Renoir's 1874 painting *La Loge* is the relationship between theatre and looking (see Figure 4). Here, a woman in a black-and-white striped silk dress leans on the railings of a theatre box. Her body is turned slightly to her left, and she stares to one side, suggesting that she is unaware of our gaze. Perhaps she is watching a performance, or she might be looking at other audience members in the stalls and galleries, or in the other boxes: it is unclear if a play is even in progress. The gold opera glasses that she holds in her right hand lie unused, suggesting that her body is on display: that her job is to show her clothes, rather than to look. While her gaze may be averted, the slight smile that plays on her lips suggests that she might, after all, know that we look at her. Her smile may be Renoir's acknowledgement that his painting is an object to be viewed, but it might also situate viewers of the painting as if they too were at the theatre, looking across the auditorium, perhaps through opera glasses, at this woman as a fellow audience member.

Behind the woman sits a man, also in black-and-white evening dress, staring through opera glasses that resemble binoculars. The fact that he looks in a different direction to her makes it even harder to work out where the stage might be, and which of them is looking in the "right" direction. He sits behind the woman, and his clothes are far less embellished and elaborate than hers, which suggests that he doesn't define himself so much by being looked at. Rather, his job is to look. The painting suggests that looking and being looked at are two activities of theatre-going that may have very little to do with watching the performance onstage. Instead, the auditorium is a place of social performance and display, in which gazes are exchanged and are gendered. Clothes are crucial for this exchange of looks, framing the woman's body as a spectacle which may compete with that

Figure 4   La Loge (Pierre Auguste Renoir, oil on canvas, 1874, by permission of the Courtauld Gallery, London).

of the stage. According to Renoir's painting, dressing-up is central to the audience's social performance at the theatre.

In the last chapter, we saw that the actor's body is produced by dressing-up, emerging as a set of shifting theatrical bodies, or modes. Renoir shows us that the actor is not the only person dressing up at the theatre. His painting imagines the auditorium as a place for the exchange of looks, or rather a place where some spectators look, and some are looked *at*, while they simultaneously look at the actor, and the actor looks back at them. The painting shows, then, that there is a relationship between the audience's dress and the actor's costume, a relationship that is centred on looking. In this chapter, I'm going to suggest that looking in the theatre can be formative: it can produce a particular attitude to clothing that makes fashion possible. The actor in costume is at the centre of this creation of possibility, opening up a relationship between dress, the fashion system and the body, promising to show us how to dress, and thereby how to do or be ourselves in the world.

What is the role of the theatre in the fashion system? We can find lots of evidence to prove that the theatre has been a site for the innovation and dissemination of fashion. In the eighteenth-century, it was noted that the actress Mrs Abington: 'as the pattern of elegance, drew to the boxes an unusual number of milliners from Tavistock Street' (cited in Price, 1973, p. 45), suggesting that actors supplied hat-makers with their ideas. Similarly, in Thomas Wycherley's Restoration play, *The Country Wife*, Sparkish – a failed wit – makes for the pit at the theatre, arguing: 'if I sat in the box I should be thought no judge but of trimmings' (Wycherley, 2001, p. 39). People who sit in theatre boxes, like the woman in Renoir's painting, are imagined to be interested only in fashion. What Sparkish fails to make clear however is whether this interest in "trimmings" is directed at the actors or at the other audience members. Perhaps it doesn't matter: where fashion is concerned, both the auditorium and the stage are important locations for the display of clothes.

However, while we can establish fairly easily that theatre has been a place to look at clothes, it is not so easy to say *why* this is the case. Why would theatres in general and actors in particular, be such important sites for the development of fashion? Perhaps thinking of the theatre as a space for display and looking might explain its role in the fashion system? As Georg Simmel has suggested, wearers of fashionable clothing need opportunities to display this clothing, because the logic of dress is fundamentally theatrical. Fashion requires an audience: 'adornment is altruistic: its pleasure is designed for the others, since its owner can enjoy it only in so far as he mirrors himself in them' (Simmel, 1997, p. 207). Wearing clothes requires onlookers, because being looked at is crucial for establishing those clothes as fashionable. Theatre, then, has played an important role in fashion's requirement for display, by being a space that is designed for clothes to be received, admired and enjoyed.

Actors have been (and still are) particularly important figures for the display of fashion, and have been considered leaders of innovations in dress at various points through history. If we employ Joanne Entwistle's definition of fashion as a form of clothing that is inextricably connected with social mobility, emphasising novelty, change and variety in a bid to 'maintain status and distinction' (Entwistle, 2000, p. 44), we can see that actors are instrumental to the development of this system. Actors in costume produce visual variety on the stage, open up a gap between the self and dress, generalise dress, rendering it desirable and imitable, and have played a key role in the promotion and invention of fashion. In doing so, actors are bound up with the economy of work and leisure, of status and dress, which is at the heart of this system.

However, there is an important difference between audience members and actors wearing fashionable clothing at the theatre. Actors pose a problem for the relationship between fashion and display, because they wear clothes in such a peculiar way. Performers are a paradox for the economy of dress. At various moments in history, actors have had very low social status, and have sometimes been considered servants (see Jones and Stallybrass, 2000, pp. 269–278). Nevertheless, their job entailed dressing in the high-status clothes of the rich. These clothes were rarely owned by actors themselves, but were often the property of patrons, theatres or the monarchy. Actors may have worn fashion, but that didn't necessarily make them fashionable. Actors then have been both the users of fashion and the uses of fashion, its workers and wearers, the subjects and objects of clothes. In this chapter, we will consider what happens when spectators and actors wear the same dress at the theatre, and we will investigate the paradox of a person of low status – an actor – dressing up in the clothing of the rich.

However, we shouldn't assume that admiring clothes has been a constant ingredient of theatre-going or that the actor has always been the bearer of fashion. After all, the relationship between the spectator's and the actor's clothing has shifted continually throughout history and between different forms of theatre. Fashion's status varies according to the arrangement of the theatre space and lighting, the production and theatrical function of costume, the developments of the textile industry, and the cultural attitudes to dress. A history of fashion at the theatre can offer us an insight into the interconnected web of social beliefs surrounding the body, costume, audience behaviour, and the economic systems of cloth, commodity and leisure. To consider fashion's role in theatre performance is to think about the potent history of actors and audiences.

In this chapter, I'm going to argue for the central role that the actor has played in the development in the fashion system, and I'm going to do this by drawing on a history of theatre. I will start by considering how the actor promotes variety and novelty in dress, and then go on to analyse the relationship between actors, patronage and servitude. I will conclude the chapter by suggesting that theatre costume works as a metaphor for the relationship between the body and identity. While this discussion dips into a history of fashion at the theatre, this history is partial and centred on the English stage (with some reference to French and Italian theatre). Rather than offering a complete and worldwide history of theatre and fashion (which would take up a lot more space than this book could provide), I'm using moments from English theatre history to claim that theatre has played a central role in the fashion system. Thinking primarily about the English theatre allows me to consider the developments and shifts in modes of theatre costume and fashion that a broader history would not. Before I examine this history, however, I want to look at the more general effects of the actor's presence in relation to clothes and to argue that actors are presented as exemplary figures onstage, which contributes to their role in the production of fashion.

Fashion and the Exemplary Actor

In his essay 'On Actors and Acting' in 1817, William Hazlitt argued that actors have the power to symbolise greatness because of their accumulation of roles:

> The stage is an epitome, a bettered likeness of the world, with the dull part left out: [...]. We feel more respect for [the actor] John Kemble in a plain coat, than for the Lord Chancellor on the woolsack. He is surrounded, to our eyes, with a greater number of imposing recollections: he is a more reverend piece of formality; a more complicated tissue of costume. We do not know whether to look upon this accomplished actor as Pierre or King John or Coriolanus or Cato or Leontes or the Stranger. But we see in him a stately hieroglyphic of humanity; a living monument of departed greatness; a somber comment on the rise and fall of kings.
>
> (Hazlitt, 1979, p. 43)

Hazlitt claims that actors, through their layering of memory and roles, become ideal and illustrative figures, capable of standing in symbolically for the qualities of greatness and mortality. We have seen this effect in the figure of Fiona Shaw in the previous chapter, whose roles reconfigured her body anew, and established her as a powerful figure within the hierarchy of classical acting. However, Hazlitt suggests that acting does not only establish virtuosity. Actors stand in for greatness more generally, becoming ideal social figures through their accumulation of roles and their theatrical accomplishments. Actors are the "hieroglyphics of humanity". How might this be? Why would actors appear exemplary figures, capable of standing in for ideal social qualities, when all they do is pretend to be somebody else? How can the impersonation of a fictional character bestow such symbolic properties on the actor's presence?

We might answer this question by returning to the semiotic approach to the actor that I outlined in the 'Introduction'. Semiotic studies of actors suggest that actors represent themselves on the stage, and then go on to represent symbolic qualities including the fictional character (see Esslin, 1987, p. 56). In other words, when actors appear on the stage, they always appear dressed in inverted commas, becoming "actors": heightened representations of themselves. This is the truism of the semiotic approach: all objects become "objects" when they enter the stage space, rendered unreal by their inclusion in the delineated world of art. However, when theatre puts inverted commas around actors it does something peculiar to their presence: it generalises them, making them appear representative of "Man" or "Woman". The invisible inverted commas worn by actors raise their presence from the individual to the representative, from the iconic to the metonymic: the actor stands in for the ideal social figure. This figure is to be admired, or indeed denigrated, but either way, the actor assumes a general rather than a particular stance on the stage.

What has this general status to do with fashion? Perhaps if actors move from the individual to the general once they enter the stage, they attain a generality that suggests that their clothes are the ideal, telling the audience: 'these are not just clothes; these are the spirit of all clothes'. Because in a theatre performance, costumes represent "clothes", they become symbolic of a series of moral, emotional and ideological qualities, and stand in for a set of broader social values. In this, we can see that theatre costume has the power to construct mythologies around garments, which may be later imitated or re-imagined by the spectator. Costumes can be meaningful in more ways than their significance for the depiction of character and narrative, as Michael Carter suggests, 'clothes are not simply "transmitters" of social meanings, they are also key elements in the business of symbolic exchange' (Carter, 2003, p. 156). The audience may enjoy the meanings of the character's clothes, but they may also enjoy the real actor (or what they think is the real actor) in the clothes, and admire how well the actor wears the clothes. Spectators do not simply see costume representing clothes on the stage; they also see it being *used*. Actors visibly *wear* their costume, and this costume is made of the same stuff as the dress worn by the audience. The figure of the actor makes the use of dress exemplary, offering ideal versions of the act of wearing clothes. The actor's art of wearing, managing and using costume is a central aspect of theatre's pleasures.

The move from the individual to the general when the costumed actor enters the stage has major implications for the emergence of the fashion system because, as Georg Simmel argues, elegance is based on the quality of generality, rather than individuality: 'what is really elegant avoids pointing to the specifically individual; it always lays a more general, stylized, almost abstract sphere around man' (Simmel, 1997, p. 208). The well-dressed person must always represent the wider social qualities embodied by fashion: 'fashion elevates even the unimportant individual by making them the representative of a totality, the embodiment of a joint spirit' (Simmel,

1997, p. 194). The idea that fashion generalises its wearer has particular implications for our discussion of actors in costume. If actors and costumes have already achieved a general or exemplary status through their inclusion in the playing space, then costumed actors may reverse Simmell's formula: the generality of actors bestows fashionability on their costumes by making what they are wearing appear to be the manifestation of the Zeitgeist. The ways in which actors wear dress onstage offer lessons in the possible manifestations of fashion, working as a sumptuary form of edification. The exemplary status of actors is crucial in establishing their role as the leaders of fashion.

However, theatre costume presents a particular problem for the study of fashion in the theatre. Certainly, there are many historical moments in which actors and audience members wore identical clothing in the auditorium and on the stage, and where actors were leaders of fashion. However, costume has an ambiguous status in its relation to the clothing of the audience. It is often unclear if the actor is the character's body, the leader of fashion or an object to be consumed by the audience. Even if actors wear fashion, it is not always the case that they can be described as fashionable. Rather, the generalised and emblematic qualities that their dress assumes in performance contribute to a fashion system in which the audience, rather than the actors, participates. Actors might be imagined as the equivalent of shop-window mannequins, or sales assistants at various points in history. Actors serve the system of fashion without necessarily being its beneficiaries. The actor is often closer to being the object of fashion than its consumer, promoting a system of variety and novelty at the theatre.

Variety and Novelty

Phillip Stubbes was a man with a problem. In 1583, all classes, sexes and races were attending the commercial theatre in London. Fearing that this mix of people would lead to a collapse of the social order, the Puritan Stubbes launched an attack against the flourishing practice of cross-dressing on the stage and fashionable dress in the audience, arguing that: 'there is such a confused mingle mangle of apparel [...] So that it is very hard to know, who is noble, who is worshipful, who is a gentleman, who is not' (Stubbes, 1973, p. 34). While Hazlitt suggests that actors can be seen as exemplary figures onstage, commentators have often been disgusted by the actor's use of fashion, and the audience's display of their own dress at the theatre. Indeed, another critic of the theatre in Elizabethan London, Stephen Gosson, claimed in 1582 that the actor's confusion of dress would infect the audience with sinfulness: 'players are masters of vice, teachers of wantonness, spurs to impurity, the sons of idleness' (Gosson, 1974, p. 177). Even Hazlitt's own claims for the actor's greatness are made in defence against the fact that: 'actors have been accused, as a profession, of being extravagant and dissipated' (Hazlitt, 1979, p. 43). Actors may appear emblematic and edifying in performance, but the contrast between their lowly social status in real life, and the kings they play on the stage, is at the heart of the social opprobrium they frequently attract.

Fundamentally, the criticisms of fashionable actors and audiences are centred on a concern for social stability. Fashionable clothes make Stubbes nervous: the difference between nobles and commoners is no longer apparent, and he cannot tell who is worshipful, so moral distinctions are also blurred. Even worse, the all-male stage of Elizabethan London involved boys playing women, and servants playing kings. What worries Stubbes is that people no longer resemble who or what they are. Gosson and Stubbes, like many anti-theatrical and anti-fashion protesters, attribute enormous power to dress and to theatre, and in some ways take the theatre much more seriously than theatre-makers do. As far as they are concerned, dress makes the man, and the variety of dress produced by the fashion system threatens to unmake men. Dress challenges the social order by emphasising change, while theatre offends by putting that changeable dress on the wrong body. Uses of fabric tear up the social fabric, while the actor's body undermines the body politic. Costume is highly formative and therefore dangerous according to the pamphleteers and protestors of Elizabethan London.

In the Renaissance, therefore, theatre costume posed a threat for a society that believed in the power of dress to communicate selfhood. Unlike the suggestion made by Gambon's portrait – that identity is distinct from the body – in the Renaissance, selfhood was located in clothes (see Jones and Stallybrass, 2000, pp. 1–15). When the shoemaker Simon Eyre dresses up in his alderman's robes in Thomas Dekker's play *The Shoemaker's Holiday*, his employee Hodge says to him: 'why now you look like yourself, master' (Dekker, 1979, p. 124) In Dekker's play, clothes make you look like yourself: there is no distinction made between the object of clothing and the self: dress invests man with subjectivity. Theatre, then, poses a particular challenge to a system centred on a direct relationship between clothes and identity. After all, if a lowly actor could play a king, or a boy could impersonate a woman, how could society rely on clothing to represent identity? Elizabeth I responded to this threat by legislating for the control of theatre and dress, through the institution of the Office of the Revels, and through the publication of the Sumptuary Laws: legislation that regulated what cloth people of different social ranks were permitted to wear (see Jardine, 1983, pp. 141–168). Anti-theatrical protestors expressed a similar desire to regulate bodies on the stage and in the auditorium.

It's often taken for granted that anti-theatrical protestors would automatically attack fashion and theatre; after all, their attacks are informed by the same moral concerns. But, it seems to me that these attacks are not distinct, but combined ones: concerns about clothing in the Renaissance are fundamentally concerns about theatricality, and this is because acting shares the logic of fashion. Actors, who have the status of servants, sometimes wear the lavish clothes of kings. At other times, however, they wear the outfits of Italian sailors, or clowns, or Jewish Venetian merchants. Actors not only wear the wrong clothes for the status and sex of their bodies, they also change clothes from role to role, shifting rank, national identity, professional identity and sometimes even gendered and racial identity as a result. In doing so, actors disrupt the rightful connection between dress and social status, making it possible to imagine clothes not as stable signifiers of self, but rather as costumes: removable, temporary, novel and spectacular. Furthermore, going back to Hazlitt's sense of the actor as emblematic and exemplary, the way the actor wears costume might suggest that this is how all clothes should be ideally used: the principle of dress as costume might be embodied by the audience too. Add the audience displaying *their* clothes in the auditorium, and we can see the Renaissance theatre as a place in which fashion first becomes possible, a place in which change, novelty and variety might become the driving logic of clothes.

It has not always been the case, however, that variety was at the centre of the logic of costume. Certainly, in the medieval period, the guild performances of mystery and morality plays were probably opportunities for the guilds to show off their wealth, including expensive fabrics and shoes. However, the guild costumes tended to maintain continuity from performance to performance: a king always wore a crown (even when in bed), the devil wore black or red, and Christ's face was painted gold after the resurrection (see Harris, 1992, p. 148). The status of guild identity could be seen in the richness of the cloth used in costumes, but it was not generally reflected in the novelty or variety of dress on the stage. Fashion was not at the heart of the logic of the stage spectacle. Rather, medieval performance emphasised a set of fixed character types through costume that did not vary hugely from year to year. We might say that the actors and the texts served the costumes, as Anne Hollander argues of ritualised and religious performance: 'the costumes are the drama, the characters are known by what they wear and any accompanying words support the clothes rather than the other way round' (Hollander, 1993, p. 238). It was less important for theatre costumes to vary or be fashionable therefore, than to retain a continuity of representation between performances and between the audience and the belief systems set forward by the texts and repertoire of religious performance.

However, as we've seen, by the time of the commercial theatre in the Renaissance, the focus on novelty and variety on the stage informed the logic of both costume and fashion. This logic could be sustained in the theatre because of a new source of clothes, through a boom in the second-hand clothing trade. Elizabeth's Sumptuary Laws meant that when servants were paid with their master's cast-offs (which were hugely valuable); they couldn't actually wear these clothes on the street. Instead, they sold the clothes to dealers (known as Frippers) who had lucrative arrangements with theatre managers (see Jones and Stallybrass, 2000, pp. 175–207). Audiences saw actors dressed in fashionable second-hand clothes previously worn by the nobility and the monarchy. The stage became a prime site in which audience members could admire and enjoy the display of fashion up close.

Stubbes' fears about the theatre therefore accidentally reveal one of the central pleasures of the commercial Renaissance theatre. These costumes were potentially very exciting on the stage: they provided the spectacle of real clothes that had previously been worn by the upper social echelons. The clothes retained the traces of their previous wearers, establishing the vestiges of wealth and fashionability onstage, a logic similar to the reasons why people pay huge amounts of money to own a dress once worn by Marilyn Monroe or Princess Diana. The clothes appear to be imbued with the status of their previous owners, in benefiting from the vestiges of a hierarchy (celebrity or royal) inscribed in the aura of the object, as Stephen Orgel suggests: 'the drama [might be . . .] a mere fiction, but its trappings were paradoxically the real thing' (Orgel, 1975, p. 6).

The theatres were also places in which the Sumptuary Laws were informally suspended and spectators also displayed their own finery. This display was especially true of rich merchants and their families, who had the wealth to purchase rich fabrics but, due to their social rank, were forbidden from wearing them in other social spaces (see Howard, 1993, 20–47). Audiences came to the theatre to display their own clothing and to admire the actors' costumes, as William Harrison complained: 'few of either sex come thither but in their holiday apparel, and so set forth, so trimmed, so adorned, so decked, so perfumed, as if they made the place a market of wantonness' (cited in Jones and Stallybrass, 2000, p. 188). The theatre was a space of imitation, in which actors' costumes emerged from the dress of aristocrats, while audiences copied the dress of the actors, and used the theatre as a means to view (and emulate) each other's clothes.

The relation between fashion and costume continued in the performances by monarchs and aristocrats in court masques. Masque costumes displayed power through the richness of their design. Designers such as Inigo Jones in England and Serlio in Italy created costumes from costly fabrics that depicted characters like mermaids, gods and decorative shepherdesses, drawn from Greek and Roman mythology, to confer past glories on the body of the royal performer (see Laver, 1964, p. 61). It was through the variety and sheer value of these costumes that the power of the monarch was made manifest. Indeed, the Office of The Revels kept a record of costumes worn in masques to ensure that they were not repeated too many times, so that the variety of the spectacle was preserved (see Halliday, 1969, p. 409). As Stephen Orgel argues, masques and the commercial stage were inverse images of each other (Orgel, 1975, p. 40). Aristocrats wore costumes that were specifically designed for performance, while their own everyday clothes were used in the commercial theatre as costume. Actors on the commercial stage wore real clothes that conferred power and privilege on a fictional character, while masques used fantastical costumes to invest real power in the aristocrat's body. Both forms of costume placed the possibilities of novelty and variety centre-stage. Clothing and costume were intricately interconnected in Renaissance performance, contributing to the development of a nascent fashion system.

However, by 1747, as far as "the Plain Dealer" was concerned, theatre's emphasis on novelty had gone too far. Now, actors never stopped changing their costumes, at least according to this anonymous letter sent to the actor – manager David Garrick, which complained that, 'there was a time when the best actors contented themselves with a new suit at each play [...] but some of the present heroes must not only have a new habit for every new part, but several habits for the same part, if the play continues to be acted for any number of nights' (anon. 1747, cited in Price, 1973, pp. 46–47). By the eighteenth century, variety had become the logic of theatre costume. Actors not only swapped costumes for each new role, they furthermore wore different costumes for the *same* role, entertaining returning spectators with a series of new and pleasurable clothes every night.

This emphasis on the pleasures of spectacle meant that it was no longer sufficient for the actor's costume to have once been worn by an aristocrat. Now, it was necessary for the costume to be fashionable in its own right. In her memoirs, the actress George Anne Bellamy recounted buying a dress from the Princess of Wales for use as a costume, repeating the Elizabethan theatre's use of second-hand clothes. However, when the dress was worn onstage, it failed to impress: 'it was not in the least soiled, and looked very beautiful by daylight, but being a straw colour; it seemed a dirty white by candle-light' (Bellamy cited in Price, 1973, p. 43). Renaissance costumes could only be considered fashionable because of their link to the status of their previous owners. By the eighteenth century however, it was not enough to for clothes to be aristocratic: now they must *appear* aristocratic within the specific conditions of the indoor theatres. As a result, actor managers such as Garrick and John Rich began to employ seamstresses to make theatre costumes that would appear suitably lavish by candle-light. Costumes moved from being references to another world that they imitated and reproduced, to becoming rich and meaningful dress in their own right – claiming a power of their own, rather than relying on the vestiges of the power of their previous owners.

The introduction of seamstresses at the theatre, and the employment of individual dressmakers by star actors, meant that actors could become the leaders of fashion. Now actors could innovate and test out new fashions on the stage, rather than simply echoing the already-fashionable members of the audience, and spectators sometimes came to the theatre just to see the clothes. Theatrical uses of clothing contributed to the fashion system *and* were attributed to the actor's power and virtuosity. Variations in costume were particularly expected of female performers, which resulted in some famous altercations between actresses attempting to wear the most fashionable clothes. Cecil Price describes a spat backstage between Peg Woffington and George Anne Bellamy over Bellamy's Parisian gown for *The Rival Queens*: 'Mrs. Woffington was so irritable that Mrs. Bellamy promised she would never wear this gown again, so on the following evening, she appeared in an even more splendid dress and Mrs. Woffington's rage bordered on madness' (cited in Price, 1973, p. 46). This story can be read as a parable for the frivolousness of actresses, but in fact it reveals how important fashion was for the assertion of the actor's power and art on the eighteenth-century stage.

So far, we've imagined theatre as a place in which actors wear lovely clothes, and audiences admire and emulate them. However, theatre was not only an arena for the display of fashion; it was also a place to critique it. David Garrick, for example, satirised the enormous headdresses worn by women at the time when he played the part of Sir John Brute in Vanbrugh's *The Provok'd Wife* in 1743: 'he exhibited a most extraordinary lady's cap, ornamented with such a plume of feathers, ribbons of various colours, oranges and lemons, flowers, etc, so formidable a toupee that the audience gave repeated bursts of laughter' (*Chester Chronicle*, 1776, cited in Price, 1973, p. 45). Garrick also parodied the foppish emphasis on fashion in the same role by: 'perching a small, beribboned modish hat on top of his wig' (Lichtenberg cited in Price, 1973, p. 52). Garrick's theatre was place in which fashions were begun, displayed and satirised simultaneously, perpetuating and regulating fashion's excesses through costume. The theatre, then, took the lead in the uses of fashion in the eighteenth century. Given that all performances took place in modern dress, with very little concern for historical accuracy, the actor was now a foremost user of clothes: demonstrating how they might be worn, and satirising their excesses (see Laver, 1964, p. 100). The distinction between dress and costume at the theatre was not between audience clothing and the actor's costume therefore, but rather between public and private dress. Dress for the social arena was strictly demarcated from the private dress worn at home, and given that theatre was a social arena, stage costumes always conformed to the public norm (see Sennett, 1976, p. 38). Even when play scenes were set in bedrooms, actors would wear only public clothing, including hats and wigs. Private clothing was rarely if ever seen on the stage or in the auditorium (see Sennett, 1976, p. 38). As a result, the logic of costume followed that of its theatrical and social situation rather that than of the fictional world. The stage worked as a two-way mirror, with audience members emulating the fashions set by actors, and actors sharing the social logic of the audience's dress.

However, while we have established the role of actors in creating a gap between clothing and the self, opening up the space for the possibility of fashion's emphasis on novelty, nonetheless it is not clear if the actor is capable of being truly fashionable. Instead, we might imagine the actor as a worker who wears clothes: a figure that exemplifies the uses of dress while not necessarily being the owner of fashion. I want to look at this paradox in the next section by considering the relationship between the actor, costume and patronage.

The Actor as the Servant of Fashion

In 1670 a performance of John Caryl's play *Sir Solomon Single* was staged in Dover for a meeting between King Charles II and his sister the Duchess of Orleans. This was a meeting between the English court and the French aristocracy, and brother and sister were accompanied by their entourage, who were dressed in the fashions of the day. The differences in fashionable clothing between the French and the English nobility led to a practical joke. The lead actor in the play, Mr Noaks, was encouraged by one of Charles's entourage, the Duke of Monmouth, to parody the current French trend of wearing short-laced coats and wide belts. Monmouth persuaded Noaks to transform his costume into an exaggerated version of French fashion:

The Duke of Monmouth gave Mr. Noaks his sword and belt from his side, and buckled it on himself, on purpose to ape the French. [...] Which upon his first entrance on the stage put the king and court to an excessive laughter; at which the French looked very chagrin, to see themselves aped by such a buffoon [...]. Mr. Noaks kept the Duke's sword to his dying day.

(Downes, 1708, p. 34, spelling modernised)

This is a story about patronage and costume at the theatre and reveals the economic status of the actor. The decision to pillory French fashion is made by the aristocrat Duke of Monmouth, not the actor Mr Noaks: it is the Duke who controls the meanings of the performance and uses his own clothes to achieve this effect. Mr Noaks functions as the central conduit of this parody, controlling the audience reaction through his appearance in the semblance of foreign clothing. Mr Noaks's virtuosity as an actor therefore works in service to the desires and intentions of his patron, and the act of patronage is manifested and made visible through the donation of clothes. However, it is his body, rather than Monmouth's, that enters the space and makes the joke, commanding the attention of the company. This story exemplifies the peculiar status of the actor's relationship to fashion. The fact that Noaks kept the sword "to his dying day" suggests that while actors might wear fashionable clothes, their relationship to those clothes is not necessarily one of ownership: their costumes are the souvenirs of a fashionable world that they serve rather than occupy. This story illustrates that the status of the acting profession has often been connected with the servant class, and the economic relationship between the actor and fashion has been determined partly through systems of patronage.

The economic relations of dress, ownership and identity can be seen in the term "to invest": meaning to dress, to give rights and privileges to and to spend money (Cambridge, 2009). In the Renaissance, as we have seen, these meanings were not distinct: clothing invested its wearer with the rights and identity of its status, and may have also functioned as a form of literal wealth. However, according to the economist Thorstein Veblen, in later historical moments when the self and clothes are considered somehow distinct, fashion is defined by its role within the economy of consumption and leisure. Clothes no longer invest the wearer with identity, but rather signal the wearer's relationship to work. In an industrial economy, like Veblen's late nineteenth century America, fashionable clothing was defined by its distance from labour: 'a detailed examination of what passes in popular apprehension for elegant apparel will show that it is contrived at every point to convey the impression that the wearer does not habitually put forth any useful effort' (Veblen, 1994, p. 105). Veblen's suggestion that fashion is determined by its relation to work is useful for a consideration of the role of the actor in the fashion system.

As we have seen in the case of Mr Noaks, actors were either literally or metaphorically dressed through patronage for hundreds of years. And, while these systems of ownership through clothing fell away by the eighteenth century, new modes of patron control emerged through the mark of the designer, director and couturier on costume in the late nineteenth century. In this, costume exemplifies one of the central paradoxes of the theatre: the ways in which dress can enable actors to take command of the stage and wield extraordinary power through performance, while their appearance is simultaneously marked by servitude. Costume has been a central means to claim the actor's body for the ownership of the patron, the king, the guild, the audience or the director. Fashion and the economics of theatre have combined to "own" the actor's body through costume. The tension between the actor as subject and object of clothing is located in the economic complexity of workers wearing fashion onstage.

The Medieval and Renaissance system of livery helps to illustrate the history of the actor's relationship with patronage. Livery was the system where owners of households were responsible for paying their servants with housing, food and clothing. This clothing bore the insignia of the household, so that employees were clearly marked by their relation to their patron. As Stallybrass and Jones argue, livery constituted identity: 'the putting on of clothes [...] quite literally constituted a person as a monarch or a freeman of a guild or a household servant. [...] The means by which a person was given a form, a shape, a social function, a depth' (Jones and Stallybrass, 2000, p. 2). Actors were liveried figures in the Renaissance, because they were members of companies owned by aristocrats: Shakespeare belonged to the King's Men for example, and actors owned a liveried outfit as part of their membership of the household of their patron (see Kastan, 1999, p. 328). Actors appear to shed this marking when dressed in aristocratic clothing onstage, but the livery system was still visible in the loans or donations of aristocratic clothes for theatre costumes. After all, the coronation robes of the king worn by the actor still bear the insignia of the patron. Actors were doubly in livery onstage: symbolically beneath their clothes, and literally through aristocratic donations and second-hand clothes. This system of metaphorical livery continued through the Restoration period and was emphasised further by the fact that the theatres were now directly owned and governed by the king: all official theatre performance was symbolically marked by a royal imprimatur (see Corns, 2007, p. 327).

By the eighteenth century however, actors no longer wore the livery of patronage. While the theatre was governed by royal command, and individual actors still had patrons, fundamentally, the audience were more powerful than individuals in determining the popularity and status of actors and their clothes. The riots over ticket prices meant that actor managers answered much more to the tastes of their spectators than to those of the nobility. As Cecil Price suggests: 'players were His Majesty's servants, but they were also the public's' (Price, 1973, p. 100). The public bestowed approval or withdrew it, and the fact that actor–managers now paid for dressmakers to make the theatre's costumes meant that box-office receipts had a greater effect on the lavishness of what the actor wore on the stage. Star actors began to achieve a status within the wider culture that moved them from the servant class to the celebrity one. However, this was not to say that actors escaped the economic peculiarities of their role.

The theatre continued to prove an extension of, and exception to, Veblen's thesis. Here is a place where clothes that are designed strictly for leisure are worn in plays that portray leisure onstage, and provide a leisure activity for the wealthy. And yet, these clothes are worn by workers – actors – and wearing them comprises the peculiar work of acting. The theatre is a place where poor people, considered servants at some points in history, wear the clothes of the rich, and set fashions for the aristocracy as part of their job. If fashion is defined by its connection to leisure, what does it mean that actors wear fashion in order to work? If fashion is defined by being worn by the wealthy, what does it mean that actors, who may metaphorically or literally be servants, wear it onstage? The social system of fashion is confused when placed on the inappropriate body of the actor. The changes of control over the actor's dress from the household to the royal patron, to the audience, and subsequently to the director, scenographer or couturier demonstrate that actors are inscribed by the economic status of their costumes. However, despite this relation to patronage, actors still assume an extraordinarily powerful role in their ability to work as metaphors for the relation between identity and clothes. Actors have not only contributed to the fashion system by emphasising novelty and variety and by making their use of dress appear exemplary. They do an even more complex job of showing audiences what clothes mean and what their relation is to the self.

Metaphors of the Self

In an 1844 melodrama *The Drunkard*, the heroine Mary tells the villain: 'But know, despicable wretch, that my poor husband, clothed in rags, covered with mire, and lying at my feet, is a being whose shoes you are not worthy to unloose' (W. H. Smith, 1844, cited in Booth, 1965, p. 29).

In Melodrama being fashionable is generally a sign of latent evil and debauchery. In an odd echo of Stubbes, the preface to one melodrama puts it: 'Let me hope that everyone will profit by our example and learn that fashionable follies are indeed fashionable vices, and that though Fashion may lead a man to the commission of many crimes, she can justify none' (Joseph Hutton, 2003, p. 1). Melodramas pitch an attack at fashion in terms very similar to Stubbes: fashion leads people astray, results in vice and is an outward sign of inner moral degeneracy. As a result, it is the villain who wears the best clothes in Melodrama, as Michael Booth describes him:

> In the later high society melodrama [the villain...] dresses [...in...] evening dress, cape, top hat, gold-headed cane, gloves and cigarette holder. (Heroes smoke pipes; cigarettes indicate a villain or villainess). Nevertheless, black remains the villain's colour: hair, complexion and moustache are tokens of his trade.
>
> (Booth, 1965, p. 20)

Melodrama provides a clear critique of the fashion system, and this is a class-based critique, which is not surprising given that the form emerged out of working class theatres and music-halls in the nineteenth century. This critique of fashion is a challenge to the injustices and privileges of the wealthy. However, Melodrama does something more complex than simply reject high fashion. If we return to Mary's outburst at the villain, we can see that the exterior trappings of wealth are rejected in favour of an interior self beneath the clothes. Mary makes a plea for the wealthy to see beneath the rags of poverty, to the heart and spirit of the hero. The class critique embodied in Melodrama emerges in a desire to distinguish between dress and identity suggesting that clothes don't matter: it's what's on the inside that counts.

However, even while the plays tried to argue that dress didn't matter, the theatrical system used to make this claim was entirely dependent on clothes. The role of the visual was central to the pleasures of the performance. The moral world of Melodrama was distinctly black and white: characters were either good or evil, and they tended to *wear* black or white to underline this fact. There was a direct correlation between the external appearance of the actor and the moral status of the character, as Michael Booth argues: 'people are true to their surface appearance and always think and behave in the way that appearances dictate' (Booth, 1965, p. 14). Costume was the outer indicator of an inner morality. Heroes wore light colours, heroines were often dressed in artfully disordered rags, while the villain (as we have seen) usually wore black. Behaviour and appearance were identical in Melodrama and the moral order was organised through clothes, and yet the plays claimed that clothes didn't matter, that it was who you really were that counted. Identity was expressed through clothes in Melodrama, just as the plays simultaneously told the audience that inner being should not be judged by outward appearances.

There is another, connected paradox in Melodrama, which is that in order to condemn the qualities of the villain – his fashionable clothes, his greed and his capitalist tendencies – the performance must first celebrate them. The villain is invariably the most attractive character – theatrically and visually – onstage, and is also invariably punished by the end of the play (see Booth, 1991, p. 160). Melodrama luxuriates in the qualities that it then rejects. There is, then, a tension between the moral message of the Melodramatic plot, and the theatrical means used to represent it in performance. Costume *is* identity, but the plays tell the audience to look beyond dress. Villains must be punished, but the audience can enjoy their fashionable outfits and their evil deeds nonetheless. These contradictions spell out the role that the costumed actor plays in relation to dress. Actors don't simply participate in the fashion system: they also enact social attitudes to the relationship between dress and identity. Actors put into practice the contradictions of a culture's approach to how to be a person in the world. The actor's generalising tendency relates not only to the uses of clothes, but furthermore to the practices of the self. A theatre form that foregrounds the moral connection between self and dress, while simultaneously telling us that we should disregard outward appearance, offers its audience a series of possibilities for ways of doing the dressed body in the culture at large.

The case of Melodrama suggests that the actor in costume can be revealing of a history of attitudes to the body, demonstrating that the location of identity is historically variable. A history of the actor helps to identify shifts in the location of the self, from clothes constituting identity through investiture in the Medieval and Renaissance period, to clothes becoming play-things for a theatrical form of identity in the eighteenth century, to dress operating as the external signifier of an interior identity in the nineteenth century. Changes in the uses of costume identify the shifts of identity from an external to an interior model. However, what is particularly notable about the nineteenth -century theatre is how the dislocation of identity from clothes leads to a greater demand for moral and historical logic in theatre costumes (see Sennett, 1976, p. 176). The nineteenth century was the era of accuracy. We have seen how costumes are viewed as an outer indicator of moral states in Melodrama. This interest in costume as a moral descriptor was also harnessed to an emphasis on historical exactitude and precision.

By the mid-eighteenth century, spectators had become critical of theatre's emphasis on the pleasures of variety over its service to logic and accuracy, as one critic asked: 'what business has a party of English footguards to attend upon a Persian emperor? [...] The persons of one single family [are] drest in the manner of half a dozen countries' (Hugh Kelly's *The Babler*, cited in Price, 1973, p. 55).The emerging desire for costume and staging to reflect narrative logic could be seen in Sheridan's 1779 play, *The Critic*. The stage's reliance on codified and decorative performance to communicate plot to the audience was pilloried through Puff's rehearsals of his new play. Puff believes that actors' gestures will communicate rich theatrical meanings, and his approach is satirised by Sheridan:

> Puff: why, by that shake of the head, he gave you to understand that even though they had more justice in their cause and wisdom in their measure – yet, if there was not a greater spirit shown on the part of the people – the country would at last fall a sacrifice to the hostile ambition of the Spanish monarchy.
>
> Sneer: The devil! – did he mean all that by shaking his head?
>
> (Sheridan, 1988, p. 178)

The theatre's taste for variety, the exotic and the gestural had begun to appear ludicrous. A thirst for accuracy transformed how costumes were designed for the stage. In 1738, Pompeii was excavated and actors, such as Garrick, were influenced by engravings of original Roman dress and art. In 1773, the actor–manager Charles Macklin produced a *Macbeth* that caused a sensation for its costumes, which were drawn from historical research. The nostalgia for a vaguely Roman past in court masques was supplanted by a desire to represent Roman costume as it "really was", and to locate plays visually within their historical settings (see Laver, 1964, p. 101).

However, while a new fashion for history emerged in the eighteenth century, it did not replace the emphasis on the visual and virtuoso pleasures of costume. Rather, history was another form of playful dress, another modish style. Historical realism worked simply to accessorise and complement the contemporary and fashionable dress of the day, and was only one of many accessories in the actor's toolkit. While references to surface truth were enjoyed as exotic spectacles, any thorough surface accuracy was greeted with boos. Richard Sennett describes how: 'in 1753, Madame Favart appeared once on the stage in the sandals, rough cloth and bare legs of a real working woman of the provinces; the audience was disgusted' (Sennett, 1976, p. 71). Accuracy was seen as only one of many tools in the variety of attractions on the stage, but was not permitted to get in the way of the visual pleasures of the actor's body. William Hazlitt's complaint in 1816, about the accurate costumes for a production of *The Distressed Mother* exemplifies this approach:

> we highly disapprove of the dresses worn on this occasion and supposed to be the exact Greek costume. We do not know that the Greek heroes were dressed like women, or wore their long hair straight down their backs. [...] It is a discovery of the managers and they should have kept their secret to themselves.
>
> (Hazlitt, 1957, pp. 99–100)

However, by the mid-nineteenth century, historical accuracy had taken hold as the theatrical and *moral* principle of the theatre. Queen Victoria, a keen theatre-goer, expressed the connection between accuracy, authenticity and morality in her description of Kean's production of *The Corsican Brothers*:

> Albert was in ecstasies for the mise-en-scene, the beautiful and numerous changes of scenery, the splendid and strictly correct antique costumes, all taken from the best works and models, the excellent grouping of every scene, the care with which every trifle was attended to, make a unique performance.
>
> (cited in Baugh, 2004, p. 320)

Victoria's description conflates accurate costumes with the pleasures of spectacle and the qualities of correctness and excellence. Now history is enjoyable, and it is also instructive. Visual accuracy is presented as a form of authenticity that produces moral insight. As a result, accuracy operates as the alibi for pleasure. The presence of historical research through sumptuous costumes permitted audiences to consume a form of spectacle that appeared serious, as well as thoroughly enjoyable. Audiences could take pleasure in the actors and their clothes, safe in the knowledge that they were *learning*, a view still in circulation about the pleasures and edifying qualities of period dramas on television, in which the historical costumes are somehow imagined to instruct viewers, by giving them insight into a superior past moment. Nostalgia and accuracy were combined in historical drama towards moral ends. As Anne Hollander argues: 'the public was [...] being trained [...] to think of the whole past as spectacular and of all spectacle as authentic' (Hollander, 1993, p. 291).

If, as I suggested of melodrama earlier, the actor is a metaphor for the wider cultural practices of the self, we might ask how the desire for surface accuracy on the stage reveals the nineteenth-century attitudes to the self. For Richard Sennett, this interest in exactitude in the theatre expressed a social anxiety about the relationship between appearance and identity on the street. The emergence of mass-produced clothing, an outcome of the industrial revolution, rendered social distinctions – so crucial for the fashion system – harder to express through clothing. Clothes now worked as a kind of disguise for the self, emphasising conformity, homogeneity and uniformity over the theatrical dress of the previous century. The role of dress was to render the body socially correct, while no longer coinciding with the identity of the person *within* that body (see Sennett, 1976, pp. 161–174). Fashion was necessary to make sure that the body could not be morally impugned, preventing accusations of impropriety. The fact that clothes betrayed so little about people on the street (after all, if all men wear dark suits and hats, how can we tell them apart?) meant that there was added pressure on art forms like the theatre, to provide an artistic space in which people could look "as they really were", a place where costume's visual accuracy was a form of spiritual authenticity (see Sennett, 1976, pp. 174–177). This desire manifested itself in the moral transparency of Melodrama, and in the surface accuracy of historical productions. Both forms provided a world: 'where you could indeed be absolutely sure that the people you saw were genuine' (Sennett, 1976, p. 176). Sennett argues that accurate dress on the stage was the expression of anxiety about unreadable appearances on the street.

As a result, we might now see in Renoir's painting, that looking at the theatre can take the form of moral surveillance. To look at the other spectators in the theatre is to judge the proprieties of their dress, to examine their countenance for the expression of correct or improper selves. Edith Wharton's novel, *The Age of Innocence*, begins with a scene at the opera, in which women seated in the boxes are viewed by the male spectators, 'the carefully-brushed, white-waistcoated, buttonhole-flowered gentlemen [...] turned their opera-glasses critically on the circle of ladies who were the product of the system' (Wharton, 1994, p. 6). The novel suggests that looking at other audience members at the theatre is an act of judgement that combines admiring fashion with moral speculation. This dimension of looking is made especially clear when Countess Olenska, a scandalous woman who has left her husband, appears in the theatre box. Olenska's fallen status is indicated by the unfashionable qualities of her clothes, being dressed in 'the dark blue velvet gown rather theatrically caught up under her bosom by a girdle with a large old-fashioned clasp. The wearer of this unusual dress, who seemed quite unconscious of the attention it was attracting, stood a moment in the centre of the box' (Wharton, 1994, p. 7). The scene Wharton conjures up suggests that fashionability and correctness in dress are allied socially with moral correctness: fashion now guarantees immunity from accusations of vice rather than, as Philip Stubbes suggested, being an expression of it. Fashion protects the body and the self from the probing eyes of other spectators. Wharton's description of the act of looking coincides closely with Renoir's depiction of it in *La Loge*: looking is a male activity and women are defined and regulated by their exposure and display at the theatre, an effect we will examine in more detail in the discussion of nudity onstage in Chapter 5.

However, while Sennett's argument that accuracy on the stage is an inverse image of anxiety about appearance on the street is persuasive, it doesn't entirely account for the contradictions inherent in many Melodramas and historical productions. As we have seen, these performances emphasise surface accuracy while simultaneously telling the audience that the surface is a lie, that it's what is "underneath" the surface that counts. The costumed actor tells the audience: "I am how I look," while saying at the same time: "my appearance does not reflect my true self." This contradiction is very common in theatre performance, as Melodrama shows us; theatre often uses exterior trappings to suggest that identity is on the inside. The nineteenth-century theatre's emphasis on surface appearance, and yet its denial of the importance of appearance, offers an expression of the tensions within the culture in its attitudes to identity and dress. The actor does not so much stand for the practice of the self, as for the manifold contradictions of a society's approach to that self. The costumed actor is a metaphor for the wider struggles over how to dress, and what dressing is for, at various moments in history.

Inventing the Self

Renoir's painting shows us that the auditorium is a space in which the actor is only one figure amid a series of social exchanges. Renoir's female spectator doesn't simply go to the theatre to watch a play. Rather, she is caught up in a series of glances that determine not only what she wears, but how she wears it and what the relationship between her dress and her sense of self might be. Similarly, when we consider a history of the actor at the theatre, we see the costumed actor busily feeding the public appetite for variety and novelty, generalising and exemplifying the uses of dress and exacerbating the widening rift between ideas of the self and clothes. We can see an actor who is bound up in an economy of work and leisure, dressing in the clothes of the rich, standing as a generalised, often objectified, conduit for the approach to fashionable dress in the audience.

In the end, the actor shows us how to dress at the theatre. But as we have seen, the act of dressing-up is deeply complicated. When actors show us how to dress, they are actually showing us how to enact our bodies and our selves. Dress isn't merely the external decoration of appearance, but rather constitutes a deeply formative metaphor for being a person in the world. This metaphor is often contradictory, doesn't necessarily add up, is frequently inconsistent and is often informed by the broader tensions and struggles in the culture over what being a person might mean or be for. Dress doesn't simply reflect these tensions: it also produces them, and the theatre has been a vital place in which the metaphor of clothing has been invented, imagined and displayed. Theatre is a place where we learn how to make ourselves through clothes.

3

Re-Dressing the Actor: Modernist Costume

In H. G. Wells' 1913 story 'The Obliterated Man', a journalist, Egbert Craddock, is forced to attend the theatre for the first time as a critic for his newspaper. His experience resembles the disorientation that we have seen in Pentheus and Count Muffat: he is overwhelmed by the: 'fantastic gestures, the flamboyant emotions, the weird mouthings, [...] and other emotional symbolism of the stage' (Wells, 1913, pp. 2–3). However, Egbert's disorientation goes further than Pentheus's double vision, or Muffat's dizziness. He finds that attending the theatre begins to infect him: that he can't help behaving like an actor. His body takes on a life of its own, entering into melodramatic poses of pity, fear and grief that are beyond his control. Egbert imagines the effects of theatre as a form of contagion:

> the acting, I saw, was too much for my delicately-strung nervous system. [...] I was giving way to the infection of sympathetic imitation. Night after night my plastic nervous system took the print of some new amazing gesture, some new emotional exaggeration, and retained it. A kind of theatrical veneer threatened to plate over and obliterate my private individuality altogether.
>
> (Wells, 1913, p. 3)

Egbert's description of theatre as a disease echoes Stephen Gosson's view in the previous chapter, that performance is transmissible and contagious, infecting the audience with its vices and its inherent untruths. However, the language Wells uses to describe Egbert's dilemma is distinctly modern. He draws on medicinal versions of the body unknown to Gosson: the idea of a nervous system, for example, relies on a relatively recent medical version of the human body. But it's more specifically the story's imaginary correspondence between the exterior conduct of the body and its interior "private individuality" that guarantees these lines could only have been written in the twentieth century. An interior self that is somehow obliterated by the "veneer" of outward behaviour, imagines identity, the body and performance in a spatial configuration that is peculiar to its time. Egbert suffers from the sense of being imprisoned by his theatrical infection, of being 'too deeply encrusted with my acquired self' (Wells, 1913, p. 5). For Egbert, the self is inescapable, but can be acquired, is formed from the outside, but is nonetheless deeply located, offering a paradoxical vision of identity that is fixed and permeable, and interior and exterior, all at once. In this, the story underlines the spatial metaphors often employed to describe how the self functions in relation to our bodies and to performance.

The tone of the story is wryly funny in the extent of Egbert's obliteration. Nonetheless, there is something uncannily familiar about his tale of woe. Perhaps in a fit of melancholy, or anger, or excessive weeping, a slightly embarrassed part of us wonders if we learnt these postures from the stage. Are we really sure that we don't behave like actors? Egbert's predicament is uncanny not because being actor-like is false, but rather because it is difficult to distinguish between the theatrical and the real. Furthermore, the story suggests that emotional states are encoded by conventions that we have learned from theatre or television or film, making it apparent that our selves may not be absolutely "private and individual". Rather, our identity may be formed through the correspondence between artistic representation, the substance of our bodies, and an interior identity that is not in fact interior at all, that is produced through the social performance of our selves. While Egbert rebels against theatre's encroachment on his sense of self: 'deep down within me I protest against the wrong done to my personality ... unavailingly' (Wells, 1913, p. 6),what we see is that Egbert's personality is in fact formed by his theatre going: it is not discreet, stable or deep down, but is rather continually reformed on the surface of his body by his exposure to art.

Egbert's contagion by theatre performance is just how artists in the early twentieth century, such as Stanislavski, Craig, Meyerhold, Artaud, Schlemmer and Brecht hoped theatre would effect, affect and infect their audiences. These artists imagined the self as unstable and the theatre as a potent site for transformation. Their approach was the outcome of a series of historic shifts in the location of the self. The peculiar spatial metaphors of identity in Wells' story reflect the idea of a divided self that emerged in the late nineteenth century. Thinkers such as Charles Darwin, Karl Marx and later, Sigmund Freud, undermined the idea that humans were the masters of their conduct and environment. Nineteenth-century Romanticism had imagined an authentic interior self that could be rediscovered and extracted from the alienating consciousness of the industrial revolution. However, by the end of World War I faith in a coherent human subject had become unfixed by the brutalities of the modern age, the shifts in time and space brought about by new technology and accelerated travel, and the fragmentary effects of new theories of the psyche and the organism of the body (see Berghaus, 2005). People were no longer masters of their own conduct. Instead, they were governed by technological, biological, psychic or economic forces beyond their control. Some theories, such as Darwin's, located the self in the substance of the body: in its genes, its evolutionary drive and its nervous system. Other theories, such as Freud's, established a self that was governed by mysterious and uncontrollable psychic forces. However, what unites these attitudes is in the ways that the self is imagined through a series of spatial metaphors that establish a set of imaginary relationships between substance, behaviour and the interior and exterior of the body.

The emerging loss of faith in a coherent human presence crystallised in new approaches to the costumed actor in Modernist and avant-garde theatre. Early twentieth-century theatre artists struggled to find version of the actor that could adequately embody the divided and fractured self, and occupy the temporal and spatial shifts in brought about by modern technology. This dilemma implicitly articulated three interconnected questions: what can an actor be, when the self is no longer coherent? What does an actor need to be in order for this new version of the self to be enacted and thought? What does the environment of the stage need to be in order for this self to emerge in the time and space of modernity? The twentieth-century stage struggled to establish a version of the actor that could stand as an adequate metaphor for the new spatial relations of identity. The living breathing virtuoso performer was now viewed as the theatrical obstacle to the representation of modern versions of identity. The solution to this problem was to be found in the invention of new forms of costume. The anxiety in the nineteenth century about the tension between clothes as revealing of self, and clothes as distinct from self, was redistributed into varying structures of appearance and truth that the costumed actor struggled to embody.

In the rest of this chapter, I will consider this struggle in three main ways. I will start by considering how actor training and scenography reconfigured the relationship between substance and the self. I'm concentrating specifically on the Naturalist movement in this section, since this theatre form was particularly focused on the relationship between surface accuracy and truth. I will then go on to examine the reinvention of the actor, and focus in particular on how costume became an autonomous object, used to produce substitute versions of the performer. Third and finally, I will consider how new versions of the self demanded new versions of beauty that were centred on the relationship between aesthetics and usefulness. Throughout this chapter, I will look at the struggles of modernist and avant-garde artists to produce a costume that could provide insight into the fractured and divided self.

Naturalism, Surface and Depth

Kostya and his fellow trainee actors in Constantin Stanislavski's peculiar pseudo-biography, *Building a Character*, are asked to pick a costume from the theatre's stock for a dramatic exercise. One of the actresses responds in the tradition of the old theatre: 'being a flirtatious young woman, she found her eyes distracted and her head in a whirl from seeing so many lovely gowns' (Stanislavski, 2001, p. 11). For Stanislavski, this woman, clearly at the whim of the instincts of an older theatre tradition, and not least the weaknesses of her sex, exemplifies the *wrong* approach to dressing-up. Her desire to amplify her own attractions through costume is judged inadequate for the demands of his radical new methods of making theatre. Stanislavski's system of performance training for the Moscow Art Theatre in the late nineteenth and early twentieth century, established a new attitude to costume essential to the actor's approach to acting. Kostya, the model-student of the book, shows us the exemplary approach, when he finds a decrepit costume in the theatre's wardrobe and responds correctly. He describes how: 'a slightly terrifying sense of fatefulness stirred in me as I stared at that old morning coat' (Stanislavski, 2001, p. 11).

Kostya's sense of fatefulness is stirred because of the psychic effects of the costume: it invades his unconscious. In language remarkably similar to that of Wells' short story, Stanislavski establishes a spatial structure of identity that is reconfigured by the formative effects of dressing-up. The costume's resonances invade the actor's interior, and reappear in the form of a purgation or fever. Kostya describes how: 'what had risen to the surface in me plunged out of sight again and I found myself once more filled with perplexity' (Stanislavski, 2001, p. 14), and: 'almost as if I were in some sort of delirium, I trembled, my heart pounded' (Stanislavski, 2001, p. 16). The imagery used by Stanislavski is medicinal: the costume is a psychic infection that reconfigures the actor's interior, manifesting these changes once again on the exterior of the body. Putting a personality on creates personality within, surprising the actor with its force: 'I was myself amazed at the brazen un-pleasant tone' (Stanislavski, 2001, p. 17), a tone which Kostya produces when performing in the coat. Like Egbert, in Wells' story, Kostya is exposed to an exterior stimulus that makes its way into his nervous system, his dreams and his unconscious, and re-emerges again in new forms of expressiveness. Stanislavski's emphasis on dressing-up as a form of psychic transition suggests that the averted gaze we found in portraits of actors dressing-up in Chapter 1 might be a peculiarly twentieth-century trope, one informed by belief in the power of costume to infect the unconscious.

However, unlike Egbert's helpless infection by theatre, Stanislavski suggests that in the actor's case, the psyche is split. The actor is subsumed by the costume's effects and yet distant from them, capable of observing and even controlling the transformation. Kostya notes that: 'I did not lose the sense of being myself. [...] While I was acting I felt exceptionally pleased as I followed my own transformation' (Stanislavski, 2001, p. 21). The costume is an external stimulus that transforms the actor's interior private self, but it is as if there is another Kostya standing at a distance from this process. The actor is a creature of instinct, responding involuntarily to stimuli, and is simultaneously a director of that instinct: 'I divided myself, as it were, into two personalities, one continued as an actor, the other was an observer' (Stanislavski, 2001, p. 21). Stanislavski draws on the modern conception of the divided self, but suggests that this division can be useful for the theatre. Actors can harness the distanced and observing side of their psyche, and use it to mediate and control their instinctive costumed transformation.

Clearly influenced by Darwin's theories of stimulus and instinct, Constantin Stanislavski developed a theatre training programme, and method of theatre directing, that centred on the actor's relation to things. He aimed to harness the actor's inner emotional landscape in the service of a reproducible spontaneity. Actors were considered to be in need of training, to be coaxed out of unruly and childish habits, and his techniques centred on disciplining bodies and their psyches. In this, Stanislavski imagines the actor as a figure who is distorted by culture and by theatrical tradition. Training will restore the actor's access to the natural, the instinctive and the spontaneous. Kostya's costume is a stimulus that produces involuntary psychic effects. In this, Stanislavski imagines the costume, the body and the self in a dynamically shifting interaction, moving between the surface and the interior of the body, governed by a distinct and watchful figure within the actor, who enables and controls these shifts.

These imaginary interactions informed a wider approach to objects in Naturalist theatre. Naturalism, a movement that emerged in the late nineteenth century, was strongly informed by Darwinian empiricism and burgeoning theories of class and the unconscious, and it rejected and reiterated the paradoxical relationship with costume that we saw in Melodrama in the previous chapter. In resistance to the nineteenth-century theatre's emphasis on spectacle and show, Naturalism refocused the audience's attention on the meanings of the fictional world of the performance, with the theatrical labour involved in creating this illusion, hidden from sight. The idea that an actor's costume might be visually pleasurable in its own right, or establish and amplify the actor's attractions, was rejected in favour of actors and costumes serving the world of the play, and the wider social truths it attempted to expose. The shared world of the audience and actor was split. The audience now occupied a distinct time and space to the performer: the audience sat in the theatre, while the actor occupied a middle-class drawing-room or kitchen. In this, Naturalism challenged the theatrical status quo, radically rejecting the culture of spectacle and fashion of the nineteenth-century stage, by employing ugly clothes, real tables and chairs and actors who turned their backs on the audience.

As a result of the desire to overcome the inauthenticity of theatre costume, Naturalism relied on a reconfigured relation to surfaces, presuming that the exposure to authentic dress and objects would produce equally authentic interior changes in both actor and audience. This approach centred on Naturalism's view of the body as corrupted by its socio-political context. The audience's job was to view and analyse this distorted body within its real social environment. This environment was most clearly established onstage by costume. Naturalist artists used clothes metonymically to suggest the distorting effects of society: the corsets, neckties, hats and shoes of the era stood in for the constrictions of bourgeois life on the stage. Costume became an outer indicator of inner deformation. Naturalist artists therefore drew attention to costume, and simultaneously encouraged the spectator to see through it, to the social truths and inner torment that lay beneath the corsets and cravats. However, their desire for scientific objectivity, using costume as an example of environment and behaviour, worked in tension with their desire for an erasure of the visible mechanics of representation. Naturalist theatre retained the visual tendencies of the nineteenth century, through its continuing focus on surfaces. While these surfaces were expected to lead the spectator to a greater understanding of what lay beneath them, with William Bodham Donne arguing that: 'to touch our emotions [...] we need not the imaginatively true, but the physically real' (Donne, cited in Baugh, 2005, p. 17), the focus on the physically real refocused and extended the cultural tensions around the relationship between surface and depth. Take, for example, George Bernard Shaw's elaborate description of the character Lady Britomart in *Major Barbara*:

> Lady Britomart is a woman of fifty or thereabouts, well dressed and yet careless of her dress, well bred and quite reckless of her breeding, well mannered and yet appallingly outspoken.
>
> (Bernard Shaw, 1957, p. 51)

Here, surface constitutes a person's inner being. Lady Britomart's contradictory attitude to her dress is indicative of her contradictory nature. However, it's unclear whether Lady Britomart's dress has made her contradictory, or whether her dress simply reflects that contradiction. Surfaces are imagined to form the interior self, and are equally merely the means to access this self.

However, while empirical thinking might have suggested that that the observable qualities of objects are somehow a means to the true, unfortunately the observable qualities of objects invariably become "untrue" when put onstage, are rendered theatrical simply through their inclusion in the frame of the playing area. The artificiality and untruthfulness of theatre may well lead to insight into another set of truths, truths that can only be found in theatre and art more generally, but the notion that real objects could preserve their reality when in performance was unsustainable on the Naturalist stage. Objects and costumes would keep on slipping from the iconic to the symbolic, from the metonymical to the metaphorical. The Naturalist movement places faith in the ability of real substances and objects to have a transubstantial effects on actors and audience, but those substances kept on insisting on becoming theatrical. As a result, while Naturalist productions focused on the trappings of the real, using three-dimensional sets and accurate depictions of clothing, the form simultaneously harboured a deep suspicion of the visual. What was important was *not* the exterior social trappings, but what lay "beneath" these trappings: motivations and forces that compelled human behaviour and desires.

Despite its suspicion of spectacle, Naturalism lingered on the visual through the richness of accuracy. The correct surfaces onstage should lead to insight into interior truth. Audiences should engage with the realness of the costume, and simultaneously see through this costume to the truth beneath it. The audience should sit in the newly darkened space of the auditorium, examining the costumes, armchairs and actors as if they were examining bacteria under a microscope. And, like good empirical scientists, they should make a diagnosis: should see beyond the bacteria to the wider disease. However, this analysis doesn't stop there: it is as if, after the performance has ended, the audience should now recognise that they are in fact infected by the bacteria that they have examined. The diseases they have witnessed – illnesses of social repression or the distortions of corsets – are in them too. Like Kostya's coat, the performance itself is imagined as a stimulus for social change, and the audience are imagined to gain diagnostic skills from going to the theatre. Theatre may not infect the spectator, as it does in Wells' story; it rather makes the audience capable of acknowledging the social diseases they already suffer.

Inventing the Actor

In 1911, the artist Edward Gordon Craig diagnosed one of theatre's primary diseases: the living breathing body of the actor. Craig viewed the actor as the obstacle for the expression of true emotion on the stage. Even worse, the actor's unruly and undisciplined body infected the stage environment with a messiness that made art impossible. He describes the actors as moving: 'as one in a frantic dream or as one distraught, swaying here and there; his head, his arms, his feet if not utterly beyond control, are so weak to stand against the torrent of his passions, that they are ready to play him false at any moment' (Craig, 1911, p. 56). The actor for Craig experiences the same delirium as Stanislavski describes. However, unlike the Stanislavski actor who is capable of observing and controlling this fever, Craig's actor is entirely powerless to master this process. Craig echoes Diderot in his conviction that the actor 'must feel as little as is necessary' (Craig, 1911, pp. 66–67), and believed that the actor should be repressed or even eradicated in order to establish a true representation of the divided self on the stage.

As we saw in the previous chapter, the actor has a tendency to the generalised and the exemplary. This generalising tendency is deeply worrying for modern artists struggling to stage a new relation between substance and self. Fundamentally, the substance of actors onstage presents a problem. How do you stage the fractured self, when that self is embodied by a seemingly unfractured actor? How can artists challenge the coherence and consistency of human presence when the actor is so stubbornly *there* on the stage? How can they escape the bourgeois emphasis on spectacle when surfaces are their primary means to elaborate insights and truths? How can they show the real, when the real is made artificial simply by including it in a theatrical performance? Inversely, how can they establish the true onstage, without the real getting in the way?

Many philosophers and artists considered the actor too real for the stage. Theodor Adorno argued that the repression of the actor's presence on the stage was the requisite for the creation of a Modernist theatre, as Martin Puchner argues: '[according to Adorno] the success of modernism in the theatre depends on the theatre's ability to resist the personal, the individual, the human and the mimetic – all of which are tied to impersonating actors' (Puchner, 2002, p. 4). Similarly, as Puchner suggests, Walter Benjamin believed that: 'the living actor becomes the obstacle for a truly modernist art' (Puchner, 2002, p. 4). Those live actors then, with all their messy presence, their unpredictability, their fondness for approval and applause, their mechanical approach to performance, (and yet their inability to repeat perfectly), their essential *thereness* for a theatre aspiring to the true, the psychic or the metaphysical: these actors were the source of the problem for Modernist theatre.

Artists responded to this problem in various ways, but one of the main solutions was to reduce the obvious presence of the actor. This was achieved by substituting the actor with objects. Craig, for example, offered two costuming solutions: the mask and the Uber-Marionette. Masks, for Craig, could overcome the realness of the actor's face, since: 'human facial expression is for the most part worthless. [...] Drama [...] takes us beyond reality and yet asks a human face, the realest of things, to express all that. It is unfair' (Craig, 1983, pp. 20–21). He concluded that masks would enable the theatre to become richer in its representation: 'the mask must only return to the stage to restore expression' (Craig, 1983, p. 23). Masks then, divert the audience away from their absorption in the messiness of the actor's humanity, towards the metaphysical insights of art. However, Craig went even further with his concept of the Uber-Marionette – a life-size puppet – that would replace the actor entirely. Puppets could establish a site of emotional projection for the spectator while erasing the uncontrollable aspects of the actor's body. Objects, therefore, do the proper work of transforming an audience, ensuring that the "correct" and "intended" effect can be achieved without the messy interruptions of the actor's presence. The shifts between interior and exterior transformation that Kostya experiences are circumvented by a theatre world completely made out of surfaces. Audiences gain insight by projecting depth onto the flattened plane of the mask or the Uber-Marionette.

Craig was echoed by the Futurists who also promoted the erasure of the actor's body onstage, with Prampolini arguing in his 1915 manifesto 'Futurist Scenography' that: 'in the final synthesis, human actors will no longer be tolerated' (cited in Kirby, 1971, p. 91). The Futurists were less concerned than Craig by the uncontrollable urges of the human body. Instead, the difficulty was that actors got in the way of their desire to develop a theatre of machines that could transform the human. Emphasising the radical times and spaces of new technologies, they created performances such as the 1925 *The Love of Two Locomotives for the Stationmaster*, whose actors were dressed in: 'two tubular metallic costumes' (Kirby, 1971, p. 93), representing trains. Prampolini, like Craig, imagined a stage entirely absent of actors and in place of the Uber-Marionette, he suggested using "actor gases" which would writhe about on the stage and 'by such whistles and strange noises, give the unusual significations of theatrical interpretations ... with much more effectiveness than some celebrated actor ...' (cited in Kirby, 1971, p. 91). Prampolini's vision almost came true in the performance *Three*

Moments in 1927, where actors were replaced by a fan, an elevator and a glowing jukebox (see Kirby, 1971, p. 93), prescient of Beckett's *Breath* in 1969, where only a mound of rubbish and the recorded sound of a human cry confronted the spectator (see Beckett, 1986, p. 369).

For Craig and the Futurists, things and machines are more capable of transforming the audience's view of the world, than the uncontrollable time-bound and stubbornly human actor. Costumes and objects offered a solution to, and substitution for, the actor. Just as belief in the coherent presence of the human/actor diminished in the early twentieth century, so the object onstage was invested with a growing subjectivity and humanity. The messiness of actors was rejected in favour of objects like masks, machines and puppets, which gained in animation and instrumentality, becoming agents in the world of the performance. Artists believed that objects could function as a medium for audience transformation in ways that actors could not.

This approach to objects informed many of the changes to theatre practice in theatrical Modernism and the avant-garde. Naturalist artists believed in the ability of accurate objects to bring about insight into wider social truths. Truth could be diagnosed through and beneath the exterior form of things. Alternatively, Craig imagined that objects, such as masks, would enable audiences to gain insight into wider metaphysical truths, arguing that: 'my aim shall rather be to catch some far-off glimpse of that spirit that we call Death' (Craig, 1911, p. 74). Here the object has no depth, not at least in the form that depth takes in Naturalism. Instead, for Craig, surfaces have a shamanistic effect, in their ability to transform the audience. Here, truth is the opposite of accuracy. The audience's gaze is imagined to bounce off the object somehow, deflected towards metaphysical insight. Antoinin Artaud, the French Surrealist, also attempted to achieve this effect, describing the experience as akin to seeing the double of the object: its metaphysical essence (Artaud, 1970, p. 37). The audience see in the mask or the puppet a second, doubled, version that turns the actor into an effigy and the actor's work into a kind of dream. Depth is accessed through surfaces that divert the audience's attention towards the recognition of eternal truths.

Indeed, the widespread uses of masks in the early twentieth-century theatre, demonstrates the ongoing investment in objects onstage. Masks, as Craig argued, controlled the actors' messy expressiveness, obliterating their faces with the blank inanimate surface of the facade. Equally, for the Futurists, masks meant that the actor could be made of the same stuff as machines and other objects, ensuring the actor's substance was made suitable for the new theatre of technology. The mask was also used as a psychic stimulus for performance. The Bauhaus dancer Mary Wigman described her response to a mask of an old woman: 'suddenly my entire body was tense, unbearably tense, my hand grasping my tightly closed coat; I was straightening, growing in a struggle within and without me [...] a rhythm forced my arm upward – the theme was born' (cited in Melzer, 1994, p. 98). In language remarkably similar to Stanislavski's, Wigman posits costume as an infection of the unconscious, and describes the body responding in an instinctive and involuntary way. In contrast to Craig's use of masks in his attempt to reduce the uncontrollable aspects of the body, Wigman and the Bauhaus made the body's vicissitudes central to their use. Masks promoted innovations in movement and became one of the predicates of the actor's body in the process of creating performance.

The non-naturalist postures produced by the masks were also imagined, as Artaud claimed, to produce spiritual insights. The Surrealist artist Hugo Ball argued that masks: ' represent not human characters and passions but characters and passions that are larger than life' (Ball, cited in Melzer, 1994, p. 32). For the Surrealists, masks provided a dissonant structure between the various elements of the actor's body, which would ideally shock the audience, making exaggerated passion visible, and expressing the horrors of the world. The mask should disrupt the audience's everyday perception of the human. Surrealist masks expressed an idea of distorted self, in order to cure the audience of their own social and psychic distortions (see Melzer, 1994). However, even as masks were imagined to embody the distortions of the modern age, they also revealed a wider set of beliefs about the location of the self. The mask positioned identity in, or on, the face, establishing a spatial structure of the self, making the face the central site of identity.

Modernist and avant-garde theatre was characterised by the replacement or fragmentation of the actor with costumes and objects. Isn't this all rather anti-theatrical? After all, repressing or indeed removing the actor's live body from the centre of the performance and replacing it with controllable and inanimate objects, sounds like something Phillip Stubbes would have wholeheartedly approved of. However, perhaps we might see in these innovations less a repression of the actor, and more a reformulation of what an actor might be. In the emphasis on nervous stimulation, or puppets, or masks, or acting gases, we can see a search for a new set of substances that might account for the drastically new versions of the human that were emerging in the twentieth century. These artists did not so much reject the actor as re-imagine what the actor might be made of. Each of these artists, in their own way, re-invented the correspondence between art, substance and the self. We can see in these projects the desire to reformulate the very stuff of the actor, and the solutions that emerged frequently centred on new uses and versions of costume. Just as Egbert in Wells' story is obliterated by: 'the natural error of supposing that the actors were trying to represent human beings' (Wells, 1913, p. 3), the twentieth-century artists established a stage in which human beings were no longer automatically represented by living actors.

In this, we might imagine objects and masks as new versions of livery. The developments in the twentieth-century theatre were underscored by the emergence of the twin figures of the director and the scenographer. These figures functioned primarily to assert an artistic and aesthetic coherence within the stage environment, even when this aesthetic emphasised dissonance and contradiction. Costume was a key means for the director and designer to communicate their ideas about the world of the play, or the environment of the stage, or the landscape of psychic divisions or political relations. As we have seen, these ideas were often manifested in the substitution or repression of the living actor by objects. The director's authorial mark was visible in the actor's substance, and the director, rather than the actor, could now lay claim to virtuoso uses of dress. As a result, actors were once again marked and controlled by the insignia of an external and invisible body. However, the mark was not that of the patron, or the audience member, but was rather that of the twin (and sometimes combined) figures of the director and the scenographer. Actors in costume – once exemplary in their moral symbolism, or their uses of fashion, or their virtuosity – now become substitute bodies for the director's vision.

As a result, the twentieth century might be imagined as the moment in which the control of the actor's presence, theatricality and labour through the livery of costume was most apparent. However, this new form of livery was almost always employed by directors in service to a set of intended effects on the audience. Wells' story of infection-by-theatre suggests that the audience may undergo a transformation through their exposure to a reformulated actor. In the Modernist and Avant-garde theatre, this transformation centred on new attitudes to beauty and pleasure. Now, the pleasure produced by beautiful costumes and actors should serve the principle of *usefulness*: they must bring about the transformation of the spectator. Beauty was no longer viewed as art's great achievement, but was now seen as the means to an end. Furthermore, the category of beauty itself was re-imagined. No longer defined by its connection to leisure and consumption, now beauty should be the expression of health, labour and usefulness. According to these artists, costumes and actors must be re-imagined to serve a radical new approach to beauty, in order to effect the correct changes in the spectator at the theatre.

Beauty and Usefulness

When Herbert Beerbolm Tree opened Her Majesty's Theatre in London in 1897, the lavishness of the wealthy audience's dress matched the lavishness of the decoration of the theatre itself, with 'short-pile red velvet upholstery on the seats, tableau curtains of similar fabric, an act-curtain resembling a Gobelin tapestry, brown-speckled marble columns, and charise-coloured draperies framing the boxes [...] and murals depicting semi-nude women in classical dress' (Schulz, 1999, pp. 239–240). Beauty was at the heart of the theatre event, but it was defined entirely as a visual experience and was strongly connected to fashionable clothing. Tree even established an additional opportunity for the innovation of fashion when he introduced the matinee performance, aimed at the upper-middle-class connoisseurs of the newly opened department stores on London's Oxford Street, who attended the theatre in the afternoon. These were the new breed of ladies who lunched. While evening dress was not required, the matinee heralded a new fashion line: the matinee hat. These hats were: 'elaborately decorated with elements typically found in a still life or table center-pieces: fruits, flowers and sometimes stuffed birds' (see Schulz, 1999, p. 245).

Her Majesty's Theatre was clearly lodged in the relations of leisure, consumption and fashion which were symptomatic of a wider attitude to costume on the stage. George Bernard Shaw's description of this kind of theatre as: 'a tailor's advertisement making sentimental remarks to a milliner's advertisement in the middle of an upholsterer's and decorator's advertisement' (cited in Kaplan and Stowell, 1994, p. 11) linked the emphasis on spectacle onstage with commercial interests off it. Theatre established a direct relationship with the fashion industry in the early twentieth century, where the clothes onstage were made by fashion designers, reported in women's magazines, and could be bought in the couture houses of Paris and London. As one reporter asked: 'can any play really be bad [...] if we gain from it a new idea for a bonnet, hat, or other feminine trifle?' (cited in Kaplan and Stowell, 1994, p. 8). Beauty in this theatre was linked directly with the commercial interests of fashion houses and the newly emerging department stores.

While it is tempting to imagine that audiences passively consumed the visual pleasures of these performances, in fact quite the opposite was true: the spectator had a very active relationship with the images on the stage. Beauty and pleasure connected watching with consuming. Rather than looking through or past the costumes, spectators (particularly female spectators) looked directly at the clothes themselves, or rather, directly at the status given to the clothes by the performance. Like the effect of

Craig's masks, their gaze was deflected, but rather than gaining meta-physical insight, these spectators were situated within the mythologies of leisure and privilege. Beauty in this form of theatre, therefore, had its uses. Stage beauty supported an economic system for which the costumed actor was an instrumental figure: both shop dummy and broker. The rela-tionship between leisure and fashion that we saw outlined by Thorstein Veblen in the previous chapter ensured that beautiful clothes were defined by their distance from work. Beauty onstage then stood for an inactive body, invested by a system of status and distinction that centred on wealth and leisure.

Craig, Stanislavski, the Futurists and the Surrealists actively rejected this form of beauty. Instead, these artists positioned themselves against the com-mercial system on which theatres, such as Tree's, relied so heavily, and critiqued the emptiness (as they saw it) of consumerism. As a result of this critique, there was a necessary reconsideration of the role of beauty and pleasure on the stage. Costume was one of the main targets in this reformulation of theatre aesthetics, and as we saw in Stanislavski's criti-cism of the flirtatious young woman's approach to dress, there was a wider rejection of the connection between fashion, commodity and the actor's allure and attractions on the stage. This move may have explained why the modernist and avant-garde artists tended to be male: fashion, consumerism and beauty were culturally associated with women, and to reject this form of theatre was imagined to somehow revitalise performance by returning masculinity to the stage. However, this is not to say that beauty and plea-sure were rejected wholesale by (male) Modernist artists. Rather, beauty emerged in new forms that were directly linked to notions of health, truth and usefulness.

This reconsideration of beauty onstage emerged at the same time as the dress-reform movement offstage, which informed the attitudes and approaches of many modernist artists. Reformers and artists shared a belief that the body was distorted and repressed by the constrictions of fashion-able dress and old-fashioned acting techniques. Oscar Wilde's claim that reformed dress styles (such as the designs of William Morris) offered 'more health and consequently more beauty' (Wilde, 2000, p. 113) is typical of the rhetorical approach. The rejection of fashion and the redesign of dress (particularly female dress) were offered as an antidote to the constrictions of commodified clothing. The fashionable body was treated as a deformed body to be repaired by new innovations in dress, just as the distorted and unhealthy actor was to be cured through rigorous training techniques or new forms of costume. As theatre artists established a series of relation-ships between self, substance and art, dress reformers also imagined the body and the self variously depending on the underlying political values of the reform movement.

The Futurists launched a series of manifestos for the revolution of fashion alongside their technological innovations on the stage. In 1914, Giacomo Balla and Vincenzo Fani decried the constrictions of modern dress in favour of clothes with a war-like disposition, arguing that modern dress was responsible for: 'the negation of the muscular life' (Balla, 2000, p. 157). They argued in favour of radically new techniques of clothes design that incorporated 'paper, cardboard, glass, tin-foil, aluminium, majolica, rubber, fish skin, burlap, hemp, gas, green plants and living animals' (Volt, 2000, p. 161). Imagining new versions of clothes allowed the Futurists to propose new versions of the body that could be made: 'nimble [...] able to [...] to surge, to fight, to race, or to charge' (Balla, 2000, p. 158). Meanwhile, in 1923 the Russian reformer Nadezhda Lamanova argued that dress should be: 'comfortable, harmonious and functional' (Lamanova, 2000, p. 174) to serve the newly established Soviet state. Again, proposing changes to dress allowed Lamanova to envision a new version of the body that was: 'active, dynamic and conscious' (Lamanova, 2000, p. 174). Just as Lamanova attributed psychic effects to changes in dress, so too Sonia Delaunay, a Surrealist costume fashion designer, argued in 1931 that the process of making clothes: 'should be based on two principles: vitality, the unconscious, and visual appeal on the one hand; craft and design on the other' (Lamanova, 2000, p. 186). All of these commentaries propose a relationship between dress and beauty, but each in turn situates a different set of connections between the body, health (or hygiene) and aesthetics. In each case, these terms are underscored by a series of implicit assumptions about the contours of the natural body, the distorting effects of fashion and the imaginary liberation of the body and the psyche through new versions of clothes.

The theatre played an important role in the re-invention of dress. It did so in part through actors taking to the stage in reformed dress, exemplifying its uses and displaying the resulting liberation of the body and the self: Isadora Duncan's neo-classical liberated dance form and dress might be imagined in this way. However, more commonly, theatre contributed to dress reform through negation. In other words, rather than showing new versions of clothes, theatre demonstrated the problems with the old forms. Fashion was employed onstage for the purposes of critique. For example, fashion was worn on the stage in Naturalism, but it was critiqued for its repression of bodies and psyches. No wonder Ibsen's plays were so badly received when they were first performed – their staging made fashion a target of criticism. The plays did not always feature the clothes of the wealthy and leisured, but often focused instead on the clothes of the middle-classes, unsettling the actor's role as a source of aspiration and exemplification. We can see the concern that this critique of fashion caused in Clement Scott's complaint about *Hedda Gabler* that: "this was still far too like Balham to be pleasant' (cited in Kaplan and Stowell, 1994, p. 46). This assault on fashion featured in the narrative of many Naturalist plays. The great dress-reformer George Bernard Shaw's play *Major Barbara*, for example, made a direct link between fashion and female passivity. In the first act of the play, the Britomart sisters are distinguished by their dress *and* disposition: 'Sarah is slender, bored and mundane. Barbara is robuster, jollier, much more energetic. Sarah is fashionably dressed: Barbara is in Salvation Army Uniform' (Shaw, 1957, pp. 61–62). By Act III, Barbara has relinquished her religious ideals and is dressed fashionably: 'Barbara, in ordinary fashionable dress, pale and brooding, is on the settee' (Shaw, 1957, p. 114). The play deploys fashion as an outer indicator of inner passivity and conformity, and suggests that wearing fashionable clothes diminishes social energy and the ability to act. Fashion was therefore utilised, but not endorsed, in Naturalism: manipulated to subversive and resistant ends. As a result, clothes themselves became one of Naturalism's objects of enquiry and the critique of fashion was one of its aesthetic and political strategies.

However, as Kaplan and Stowell argue, *Hedda Gabler* survived the wrath of many audience members and proved to be the most popular of Ibsen's work in England due to Hedda's upper-class status and fashionable clothes. They argue: '*Hedda Gabler* became the acceptable face of Ibsen for spectators weaned on a diet of Dumas, Scribe, Augier and Sardou. No matter that Hedda's surroundings were part of a calculated assault upon the values and prejudices of just such viewers, the play's surfaces were in their own right enough to make claims upon the sensibilities of its public' (Kaplan and Stowell, 1994, p. 46). Somehow, even when fashion was being critiqued by the play's message, its existence on the stage was enough to mollify the audience and the critics. According to subsequent artists, working in the avant-garde, Naturalism did not go far enough in its critique of fashion, because it was still bound up with the systems of pleasure and beauty that it attempted to overturn.

In answer to this problem, the abstract costumes of the Bauhaus or the Surrealists presented the body as a distorted and mutant expression of the age, metonymical of a larger artistic and political despair at the distortions of fashion and the brutalities of the society it stood for. As the Dadaist artist Hugo Ball put it: 'the horror of our time, the paralysing background of events, is made visible' (cited in Melzer, 1994, p. 32). However, as in Naturalism, the logic of these costumes was informed by the fantasy of a body that was not visible on the stage. There was a melancholic yearning built into avant-garde costume, a yearning for the utopian body. In order to achieve a sense of distortion, the design of these costumes relied upon the idea of a pure, healthy and un-contorted body. After all, we could not see costumes as disfiguring unless we could picture an alternative. Like the dress-reform movement, these costumes drew on the fantasy of a pre-body: a body that existed before the deformities of modernity. Rather than this undistorted body occupying the costume, in fact it was a spectre that floated on top of it, a fantasy that was the outcome of the clothing. The design of the costumes was informed by a desire for a Romantic liberated body, and filled with despair at its impossibility.

As a result of these challenges to fashion onstage, aesthetics in the theatre became utilitarian. Beautiful clothes were no longer considered sufficient in themselves: the logic of costume was now located in its sympathy with other scenographic elements, in its revelation of eternal truths, or in its production of social, spiritual or political transformation in the spectator. The utility of beauty was a particular feature of the Political Theatre movements in Russia and Germany, which established new systems of pleasure onstage, without necessarily emphasising fashionable dress. The theatre and film-maker Eisenstein, for example, was very deliberate in his use of "attractions", arguing in 1923 that theatrical pleasure would to subject the audience to: 'emotional or psychological influence, [... which] provide[s] the only opportunity of perceiving the ideological aspect of what is being shown, the final ideological conclusion' (Eisenstein, 1995, p. 88). The Russian director Meyerhold echoed Eisenstein in his argument for beauty on the stage in 1929: 'we must understand clearly what we mean by beauty and reject all beauty that is not utilitarian' (Meyerhold, 1995, p. 100). Beauty does not suffice for its own sake, therefore: it should be used to engage the spectator with the task of critical labour and political critique. Equally, political artists promoted new visions of beauty, repositioning previously marginalised dress. Proletariat factory overalls, or agrarian folk dress, were viewed as worthy alternatives to the classical traditions of beauty on the stage, which was dismissed as the result of an anachronistic class system (see Braun, 1969, p. 184). Costume now framed actors as labourers or peasants, who mediated the meanings of contemporary culture, the new world order, and new technologies for their audience.

In the Russian director Vsevolod Meyerhold's production of the *Magnanimous Cuckold* in 1922 the actors wore overalls designed by Irina Popova, 'the characters all wore loose-fitting blue overalls with only the odd distinguishing mark such as a pair of red pom-poms, an eyeglass or a riding crop' (Braun, 1969, p. 184). Wearing overalls onstage was a practice shared by many Russian socialist theatre companies such as Blue Blouse, whose name referred to the worker's uniform. The initial impression is of course, an alliance between the actor and the worker: a recognition of the theatre as a form of labour. Overalls present "worker chic" onstage. This may have been a politic move in a post-Revolution moment, where theatre was criticised for being bourgeois and decadent. Dressing the actor as a worker suggests that theatre is a valid form of labour for the new Soviet state. The vision of the actor-as-worker was also reflected by the training methods of Meyerhold, whose approach to the performer's body was to render it machine-like through the repetitive exercises of Biomechanics. Unlike Stanislavski's system, Biomechanics engaged the actor's musculature and vocal cords in order to prepare it for the labour of acting. Beauty was now established onstage through an active, labouring and disciplined performer, doing the kind of theatrical work that is made possible by workers' uniforms.

Furthermore, actors are made uniform by wearing uniforms. As we have seen in the previous chapter, the relationship between theatre and the fashion system in the eighteenth and nineteenth centuries shored up the star system, establishing a theatrical hierarchy that was constructed through clothes. Using overalls as costumes, on the other hand, attempted to ensure that the audience would engage with the performers as a collective, and thereby banish the nineteenth-century bourgeois system that had relied so heavily on costume. Overalls would deflect the spectator's focus away from an admiration for individual performers' beauty or virtuosity, out towards an emphasis on the merits of the collective performance. Spectators would be refused full emotional identification with characters and the narrative in order to retain an engaged understanding of the ideological context of the performance, and the blue overalls were therefore essential for the production of an active and critical response in the audience.

Similar to the approach of Craig and the Futurists, political theatre artists also established a particular relationship between the body and objects. Masks were frequently used in political theatre. However, unlike the metaphysical dimensions of masks in the work of Craig and the Bauhaus, here masks presented and invented versions of social archetypes for a new world order. The company Blue Blouse, for example, viewed masks as representations of social roles: 'Blue Blouse uses masks for positive and negative types as decided by the new world and Soviet economy: Capitalist, Banker, Premier [...] Menshevik and Social Revolutionary [...] Female Worker [...] and many others not yet entirely defined' (Blue Blouse, 1995, p. 182). Masks then provided the audience with an imaginary space for the production of new and ideal social identities. However, here masks were not just representations of faces: now, the mask is a full-bodied costume. Clothes are masks, enforcing social roles and status on the body. The face was not located as the site of the self in political theatre therefore, but rather established in the entire body, and the collective body emerged as the ideal model for identity.

Objects, then, were a means to re-situate attitudes to identity and the body within a broader political context. Meyerhold's collaborator, the playwright Vladimir Mayakovsky, took the new role of objects in the world order literally in his play *Mystery Bouffe*. At the end of the play, the workers ("the Unclean Ones") make their way through Heaven and Hell, and come to a utopian futurist city, where they are greeted by objects such as hammers, bread, salt and needles (see Mayakovsky, 1968, p. 166). Written just at the end of the Russian Revolution, the play presents a utopian vision of the technological city, where genuine social transformation seems possible. Objects are at the centre of this utopia, and they come to life, animated by new social relations. The things onstage are given equal subjectivity to the human characters and are posited in a relation of interdependence that is finally free of the inequalities of capitalism (see Mayakovsky, 1968, pp. 169–170).

Mayakovsky's play suggests that objects have been deadened by capitalism, and he literally animates them in honour of a new political order, in which the human relations with objects is re-energised as a form of salvation. Things, previously emptied of their meanings by the vacuity of commerce, and deadened by old systems of beauty, are now beautiful and animate, alive and pleasurable once more. Synonymous with their challenge to the hierarchies of beauty and objects on the stage, Meyerhold and Mayakovsky interrogated the hierarchies involved in making costumes backstage. We saw how Meyerhold critiqued the relationship of the dressing room to the stage space in Chapter 1, and we can now recognise that this critique was informed by a wider political interrogation of the systems of creating theatre. He and Mayakovsky re-thought the means of costume production. According to the Prologue of *Mystery Bouffe*, actors should no longer appear in livery made by lowly tailor and seamstresses: now they should make and own their own clothes (see Mayakovsky, 1968, p. 100). According to Mayakovsky, actors should no longer be clothed by the inequities of patronage or livery. To challenge the unequal hierarchies of ownership, tailoring and acting of the old theatre, is to challenge furthermore the artifice and untruths of its stage. Now actors wear overalls and what the audience see is an exemplary ideological relationship between pleasure, labour and the means of production. Beauty and truth are the outcomes of a new form of aesthetics that is based on reconfigured hierarchies found both in the world and backstage at the theatre.

This ideological interrogation of the power relations implicit in clothing and aesthetics continued in the work of the German playwright and director, Bertholt Brecht. In Brecht's *Mother Courage*, for example, boots are worn as part of the actors' costumes, but they are also key commodities for Mother Courage's trade during the war. Boots are taken off by actors and sold within the fictional narrative. Yvette's red boots are part of her trade as a prostitute, and bolster the economy of sex and bodies during wartime. The red boots, their uses by Kattrin, their movement through the play, implicate clothes and shoes within a wider economic system that is centred on the exploitation of human bodies: soldier's bodies and women's bodies (see Brecht, 1955, p. 25). While the economic presence of clothes works at the level of the fictional narrative, it corresponds with the actual economic function of the costume offstage: boots are also worth something to the theatre, are bought and sold in the outside world and are part of the system of capitalism. Brecht used a strategy similar to that of Naturalist theatre: he established uses of clothing onstage in order to critique them. However, this critique was levelled less at the distorting effects of clothing on the body and psyche, and more at the wider power relations of production, consumption and exploitation.

Similar to Meyerhold and Mayakovsky's critique of the hierarchies of creation in the theatre, Brecht emphasised the beauty of the craftsmanship that went into the construction of props and costumes: 'particular care was taken over the props; good craftsmen worked on them. This was not so that the audience or the actors should imagine that they were real, but simply so as to provide the audience and the actors with beautiful objects' (Brecht, 1964, p. 213). Craftsmanship is a beautiful act: the labour of making costumes, and the labour of wearing them onstage are both foregrounded as worthy of aesthetic appreciation. Whereas the high fashion of the nineteenth-century stage required a distinction from work, now the work in making clothes is the location of beauty. A new body for a new world, and a new theatre form, demands a new version of beauty. Ultimately, for all these artists, beauty is to be found in the audience's transformation.

Re-Imagining Costume

Returning to Egbert in H. G. Wells' story, we find that his transformation demands a new set of clothes. His obliteration by theatre has influenced his demeanour so much that his tailor insists on a freshly flamboyant suit.

My tailor even enters into the spirit of my disorder. He has a peculiar sense of what is fitting. I tried to get a dull grey suit from him this Spring, and he foisted a brilliant blue upon me, and I see he has put a braid down the sides of my new dress trousers. My hairdresser insists upon giving me a wave.

(Wells, 1913, p. 6)

Poor Egbert! His substance has been changed so much by going to the theatre that his tailor and hairdresser insist on dressing him in a cutting-edge suit and hairstyle. The message of Wells' story works on the same principle that the artists of the early twentieth century were forced to confront: that shifts in the attitude and demeanour of the body require new versions of costume.

Modernist costumes were actively transformative for how theatre and the actor could be imagined. The reconfiguration of costume enacted the changes in the actor and caused them to take place: they brought new versions of actors into being. Modernist and avant-garde artists created costumes that constituted radically new versions of substance, self, depth, appearance and truth on the stage. Costume was their means to reconfigure what the actor was made of, a way to redraw the boundaries of the self, and to re-imagine the relationship between actors and objects on the stage. Infection by theatre was the aspiration of these artists, for whom the transformation of the audience was the greatest form of beauty. Costume was the means to create this infection and to embody insights into how to become a new person for a new world.

4

Cross-Dressing: Authenticity and Identity

In the 1999 film *Shakespeare in Love*, Simon Callow plays Tilney, the Master of the Revels, who learns of Gwynneth Paltrow's transvestite disguise when she performs Romeo in the first ever production of Shakespeare's play. He initially mistakes the real boy player for a woman, fumbling for female genitals, and finding a penis. He later accuses Paltrow, who is now dressed as Juliet, bellowing: 'that woman is a woman!' (Norman and Stoppard, 1999, p. 146), a line designed to get a laugh from the audience. "Real" women are banned from the stage in the Renaissance, and it is Tilney's job as Master of the Revels to enforce this law. His explosive reaction is centred on his anxiety about maintaining the balance between actors and their roles at the theatre. However, the joke is established through the film's audience's ability to distinguish between the real and the illusion far more easily than Tilney can. To mistake the boy player for a woman, when we can see that he is so clearly not one, seems ludicrous. The film makes a joke at history's expense: Elizabethans might fear the effects of real women performing on the stage, but we don't. The joke buried in Callow's line laughs at the notion that a woman might be anything *but* a woman, taking delight in the stability of the bodies beneath the clothing. Indeed, the film ultimately concludes with a production of *Romeo and Juliet* in which a woman (Paltrow) plays a woman (Juliet). This, the film tells us, is how theatre *should* be, and the emotional identification of the audience (we see lots of shots of spectators weeping) suggests that this modern-style performance, in which the actors play people like themselves, is far more truthful than the cross-dressed stage.

However, I wonder if the laughter at Callow's line also belies an anxiety that is at the heart of this comic moment, an anxiety about the distinction between actors and their roles? The film repeatedly assures us that the bodies it shows are stable and immutable, continually playing shots of the unwinding of the sheet binding Paltrow's breasts, in order to guarantee that her "real" female body has not been changed by her male costume. The film's dogged insistence that cross-dressing makes no difference to the actor, reveals an anxiety about the possibility that those bodies might not be quite so stable. The film's need to reassure us that Paltrow still has breasts, and the boy player still has a penis, might actually emerge from the film's concerns about the formative effects of acting. The audience laugh at Callow's line from the safe perspective of a stable world, a stable world that the film anxiously asserts through the act of cross-dressing.

Indeed, Callow's line might tell us something about how we look at actors more generally. Is this not the line that spectators utter metaphorically when they sit in a theatre and watch a female actor play a woman onstage? Through their acceptance that "that woman is a woman", spectators might produce and agree on the gender of the actor in performance. Inversely, when watching cross-dressed performance, the audience might say, "that man is a woman", or, "that woman is a man". And, as they sit in the auditorium for the length of the production, they agree to believe this statement, while also seeing doubly the "man as a man" or the "woman as a woman". Perhaps, when spectators leave the theatre they believe that those "men" and "women" will go back to their dressing rooms, take off their costume and make-up, and change back into their rightful sexed identity. But, perhaps they also leave with the faint suspicion that actors have been altered by the act of dressing-up.

We saw in Chapter 1 that there is often a desire to distinguish between "real" actors and the roles that they play. Cross-dressed actors foreground this distinction. After all, cross-dressing makes the difference between the actor and the role explicit. In order to know that we are watching cross-dressing, we must see that performers are not what they play. Costume must appear *as* costume, separate from the performer's "real body". The ability of the audience to make this distinction is structured by power relations. The gap between the performer and the costume often constitutes a gap in status as well. After all, dressing-up can sometimes entail dressing-down: performers may impersonate characters that have less social power than them, and this status-gap is often at the centre of the pleasures of the performance.

The heightened qualities of identity established by cross-dressing can offer us an insight into the power relationship between representations of identity onstage, and social relations off-stage. After all, crossing is established through absence as well as presence: actors are substitutes for identities that are not their own. By taking on the role of substitute or surrogate, cross-dressed actors often stand in for the fantasies, desires and anxieties of their social moment. However we can see that the *absences* on this stage reveal these fantasies just as clearly as the presences: the bodies that *don't* appear can point to a culture's fears about certain kinds of identities. Tilney's fears about women playing women are a case in point. The real and the illusion are not simply distinct modes within the cross-dressed actor's appearance: their relationship is fundamentally bound up with power structures that have potentially political effects on the actor, on the audience and on the wider community that is being represented in performance.

Cross-dressing is often imagined to be solely about gender. However, the theatre has been a place for a plethora of crossings, such as stage Irishness or Orientalism, which are structured by relations of power. In this chapter, I am going to concentrate on a mode of crossing that is primarily concerned with racial identity: blackface minstrelsy. Minstrelsy is the historic practice of white performers blacking up their skin and hair in order to represent black people on the stage. This is a form of crossing that is made possible by make-up as well as costume. Make-up has been a neglected issue in this study, and it really demands a book of its own. This chapter, then, is an inadequate engagement with its complexities, but does go some way to show the peculiar effects of make-up on the actor's identity. After all, make-up appears as if it is fused with the actor's appearance, and it is hard to distinguish between it and the borders of the body. Even though it can be taken off, it may appear indelible, since it looks like skin. Make-up unsettles the distinction between the real and the illusion. It has the same but more condensed effect as costume by remaining perceptually indistinct from the actor's body, yet resisting total absorption into that body.

The differences between costume and make-up can be seen in Jack Gill's commentary on the difference between gendered and racial crossing onstage. Gill argues that blackface and cross-gendered performance are not equivalent, since: 'borrowing the socially constructed meaning of clothing may illuminate and challenge the socially constructed meaning of gender; blackface in contrast borrows an essential aspect of another race, which cannot be changed at will' (Gill cited in Senelick, 2000, p. 300). Gill is right to point to the asymmetry of cross-racial and cross-gendered casting: their effects are not identical, although we would need to place these crossings within specific socio-historical contexts in order to work out what those effects were. However, Gill bases his claim on a set of assumptions about gender and race by arguing that the clothing codes of gender are "social", whereas race is "natural". He assumes that cross-gendered performance invokes an identity that can be changed at will, whereas skin colour (or make-up) signifies an aspect of race that cannot be transformed in the same way. We could contest Gill's statement, by suggesting that shifts in gender might be just as hard to achieve as shifts in racial identity, or by inversely suggesting that skin colour might mean different things in different contexts, and might not necessarily be an unchanging aspect of racial identity, as Elizabeth Abel argues: 'Rather than being a constant, colour [...] varies with positions in discursive exchanges' (Abel, 1997, p. 129).

However, I think fundamentally the problem for Gill is that the difference between cross-gender and cross-racial performance is located in the difference between costume and make-up. It is not that gender can be changed more easily than race, but it may be that for an audience, costume feels as if it can be changed more easily than make-up. If make-up looks like skin, it convinces us of its permanent state, even if we know that it can be removed. Make-up seems to modify the actor in a "real" way, and it is in the relationship between this effect of the real, the illusion of the performance and the assertion of the authentic body of the performer beneath the make-up, that the political effects of blackface minstrelsy emerge. Of course, make-up, specifically blackface, indicates its reality or removability, variously depending on its theatrical uses and context. There is a world of difference between the nineteenth-century minstrel make-up on the American stage and its appearance in productions by the experimental theatre company, the Wooster Group, or in Jean Genet's play *The Blacks*. This chapter will investigate the variety of make-up's effects by looking at a range of its uses, contexts and histories. I'm going to consider the various ways in which crossing-over might figure the relationship between the real and the illusion onstage. To do so, I will begin with a history of blackface minstrelsy in the nineteenth-century America, and go on to think about the heritage of minstrelsy in case studies such as performances of *Othello*, Ntozage Shange's *Spell No. 7*, Eugene O'Neill's play *The Emperor Jones* and the staging of O'Neill's work by The Wooster Group.

Dressing-Down: Blackface Minstrelsy

Let us look at an image of cross-dressing. Here is an 1862 photograph of Joseph Murphy (see Figure 5). What do we see? Murphy is turned away from us, facing to his right and he's dressed in a frilly white dress, with matching white flowers in his hair. He possibly wears a black shirt beneath the dress that covers his arms (it's hard to tell in the picture), and he's wearing big black boots. His face is blacked up, and perhaps his hair is too, and his mouth is outlined with white make-up. His gaze is thrown upward, making the whites of his eyes more pronounced, and his expression is hard to read. Are his eyes thrown up, like his leg, in a fit of playfulness or

Jos. Murphy
1862

Figure 5   Joseph Murphy Cross-Dressed (Anon. photograph, 1862, by permission of The Harry Ransom Research Centre).

wistfulness? Do his up-cast eyes signal that he is representing a demure young black girl, or are they simply up-cast to highlight their contrast with his black make-up? Are his boots a sociological sign of the girl's poverty, or are they more like clown shoes, designed to interrupt the image by distorting the lines of the girlish body? Is Murphy supposed to look attractive or comical? Furthermore, how many "crossings" has Murphy undertaken? What is his "real" body beneath the costume and make-up?

We can probably assume that Murphy is white, given that he has blackened his skin with make-up (although we can't be absolutely sure: our assumption is created *by* the make-up rather than our ability to see around it). We can also probably assume that he is male and pretending to play a girl, which is suggested by his name, and by the size of his feet (size that is created by the boots, which could be artificially large) and the awkwardness of his feminine pose. (Again, we can't absolutely be sure that he's male, but we can assume it based on how the costume is used.) Here, therefore, the costume and make-up want to tell us that this performer is *not* the image he represents. Furthermore, his surname, and the date on the photograph, 1862, suggests that he could be an Irish emigrant, since there was a huge wave of emigration to America as a result of the famine in Ireland in 1845. We might well ask, if Murphy is an emigrant, then why would he be found performing, in black make-up and a woman's dress? And why on earth would an audience want to watch him?

The answers to these questions are located in the historical context that informs the relationship between the real and the illusion in this picture. After all, this image clearly happened in a specific time and place, and we need to establish the context in order to interrogate the possible effects of the performance. Minstrelsy evolved in the early to mid-nineteenth century in America, and was a highly popular musical and variety form. It was performed predominantly by ethnic workers, recently arrived in America, such as Irish, German, Italian and Jewish immigrants, who were often marginalised and repressed by the "native" white communities already living in the States (see Roediger, 1991, pp. 115–133). Performers wore black make-up on their faces in order to mimic African Americans in performance. This make-up was originally made through the use of burnt cork, and the performers used red make-up to over-emphasise the size of their lips. The performers didn't simply mimic blackness; it was specifically the field slaves from the plantations in the Southern states of America who were the target of the representation. In imitating these slaves, the minstrels created distorted images of black bodies by wearing oversized and fantastical versions of their clothing. Minstrel characters were divided between the comic and violent clown figures who spoke in a broad dialect, and the interlocutor: the upper class and genteel black figure, who spoke with exaggerated correctness (see Twain, 2003, p. 92). The aim of the minstrel show was to make audiences laugh at black identity, through the use of exaggerated and grotesque costumes and make-up and slapstick depictions of violence.

However, the complex effects of the minstrel show can be seen in Mark Twain's description of minstrel slapstick as a 'happy and accurate imitation of the usual and familiar negro quarrel' (Twain, 2003, pp. 92–93). This claim is frequently repeated in descriptions of minstrelsy in this period: white audience members considered blackface performers "authentic" representations of black people. The effect of this belief in the authenticity of the depiction of blacks as musical, instinctive, violent, lascivious and stupid was to mediate the white view of black people outside of the theatre. Minstrelsy became a self-fulfilling prophecy: white audiences learned to "look" race at black people through the representations of blackness they saw on the stage. Furthermore, it's possible to suggest that black people themselves began to internalise this imagery of blackness, finding that they had to perform this model of blackness for a white culture, in order to be accepted. As Eric Lott observes of the formative effects of blackface minstrelsy: 'It was hard to see the real thing without being reminded, even unfavourably of the copy, the "cover version" that effectively did its work of cultural coverage. Nor, just as surely, could the copy be seen without reminding one of the real thing' (Lott, 1993, p. 115).

The effect of minstrelsy on black identity was formative, in how whites saw and treated black people, in how black people saw themselves and, most directly, in the race riots and lynching that often took place after minstrel performances. As Eric Lott points out, some racially motivated rioters used blackface as a disguise and as a political statement: 'during the 1834 Philadelphia race riot [...] some of the anti-abolitionist rioters who attacked the homes of well-to-do blacks, burned black churches, and destroyed racially integrated places of leisure, wore black masks and shabby coats' (Lott, 1993, p. 29). Performing in blackface had a material as well as metaphorical effects on black identity; not only through the mediation and construction of race in performance, but also in the lynching and race riots which frequently followed minstrel performances. Minstrelsy shows us that the relationship between the real and the illusion is not always an abstract concern on the stage that ends when the performance is over. Illusion can have direct and lasting effects on the absent figures it represents.

This historical account suggests that what we see in the photograph is that Joseph Murphy is an emigrant minstrel performer in the nineteenth-century America, playing a clownish version of a black girl. We might now see that the purpose of his impersonation is to mock black identity. However, this mockery feels like an inadequate explanation for the photograph. Is mockery really the only motivation for the act of blacking up? We might ask what social advantage Murphy gained from erasing the appearance of his own skin in favour of blackness. In other words, what is the power relationship between the real and the illusion in this picture? When we ask this question, it becomes apparent that accessing the real is difficult. We might invoke what we imagine to be Murphy's "real" gender or racial identity, in contrast to the represented gender or race that we see depicted in the photo. However, as we have seen, it's difficult to be absolutely sure what those real identities are, since we tend to find out about them *through* the costuming, rather than separate from it. Furthermore, we might think about how Murphy deploys the "real" as part of his own performance, in how his boots emphasise the size of his feet, for example, or in how he so clearly artificially imitates femininity. Murphy's use of costuming suggests that he needs to assert his real body, in order to make it very clear that he isn't what he plays.

We might begin by considering this deployment of the real in order to assert a distinction between character and role by acknowledging that in the 1860s, when Murphy was performing, the Irish were considered "coloured" (see Roediger, 1991, pp. 133–167). The assertion of whiteness by minstrels was intricately connected with the racial hierarchy in the nineteenth century, which situated blacks at the bottom of the scale and immigrants such as the Irish, not much higher up. Both the Irish and the black community were portrayed in cartoons and caricatures with monkey or ape-like characteristics. In order for Irish emigrants to climb the class ladder in the United States, to gain greater social power, it was necessary to achieve whiteness first. David Roediger has argued that: 'blackface minstrels were the first self consciously white entertainers in the world' (Roediger, 1991, p. 117). Racial denigration and class envy were intertwined in the minstrel use of black make-up: the black mask erased ethnic differences between immigrants, and most importantly, it established a distinction between these immigrants and African Americans. In order to achieve power in the culture, immigrants found that they had to gain the appearance of whiteness first, and they attained this whiteness, ironically, by painting their skin black. For the immigrant performers who played minstrels, the act of blackening their faces, and ridiculing and lampooning black identity produced the fantasy of a white skin beneath the make-up, a whiteness that was very clearly *not* black, or even coloured. The suggestion in Murphy's photograph that he is *not* what he plays is crucial for our belief in his whiteness underneath his black make-up. Our sense of Murphy's body is formed through his costume and make-up: his whiteness is an outcome of the photograph. The blackface image produces another image by default: the image of an ideal white body that is the inverse of what Murphy portrays.

Furthermore, this photograph shows that crossing one mode of identity involves crossing many others. Murphy is not only crossing from white to black but also from male to female, and from Irish to American. These crossings don't remain distinct in the photo we don't look at them one at a time. Rather they, as Anne McClintock suggests, form: 'intimate, reciprocal and contradictory relations' with one another (McClintock, 1995, p. 5). In other words, the representation of blackness in Murphy's image is intricately related to his representation of femininity and American identity. In minstrelsy, categories of identity emerged through each other: ethnic skin was painted to resemble black skin, in order to imagine and invoke white skin. Men crossed over to female roles and also crossed class divides by playing upper-class black figures. Immigrants from all over the world pretended to be American, situating their impersonation specifically within the black American slave body. Anne McClintock argues of the racial hierarchies invented in the nineteenth century:

> The rhetoric of race was used to invent distinctions between what we could now call *classes*. [...] The rhetoric of *gender* was used to make increasingly refined distinctions among the different *races*. The white race was figured as the male of the species and the black race as the female. [...] Similarly, the rhetoric of *class* was used to inscribe minute and subtle distinctions between other *races*.
>
> (McClintock, 1995, pp. 54–55, italics original)

However, McClintock also warns that these interrelated identities are not symmetrical or interchangeable. To assume, for example, that the parodies of women and blacks in minstrelsy had the same effects on their absent targets, is to erase the questions of class, economics, history and racial and gendered hierarchies between, and within, these groups. White women and black women might have shared the same gender, but did not have symmetrical social status in nineteenth-century America, while black men and black women also occupied different and unequal social positions. We must always keep in mind the questions of power and hierarchy when examining how multiple identities are crossed and constructed on the stage.

However, within these multiple crossings, might it also be possible that Murphy's image is supposed to be attractive: that just as we laugh at this girl, we might also desire her? Even when the image produced by cross-dressing is clearly intended to scorn the identity it represents, there might be some confusion, some contradiction and some anxiety in the image, which might be worth considering further. Part of minstrelsy's effectiveness in denigrating the bodies of black people, lay in its ability to "fix" the qualities of black identity through the performance of stereotypes. Homi Bhabha has suggested that stereotypes establish the fantasy of timeless ethnic identity. We can see evidence of this in Joseph Murphy's photograph. The black girl he portrays is fixed by the image he creates: she has no psychological complexity or ability to change: Murphy is in control of the meanings of black feminine identity. However, Bhabha argues that this need to fix identity through the use of stereotypes belies an anxiety about difference, in this case, the difference of black identity: 'the stereotype is a complex, ambivalent, contradictory mode of representation, as anxious as it is assertive' (Bhabha, 1994, p. 70). Bhabha suggests that cultural stereotypes are a sign of anxiety, that the need to fix another person's identity is a sign that we are anxious about that identity and its power. Rather than seeing Joseph Murphy's stereotype of a young black girl simply as a "misrepresentation", we should also consider the anxiety that his image expresses, and what this image might tell us about a white culture's fear of black identity.

The minstrel show therefore simultaneously produced blackness and whiteness: blackness in the grotesque caricatures, which subsequently mediated how black people themselves were seen, and whiteness in the homogenising effects of the burnt cork mask. The ways in which whiteness was produced through minstrelsy suggests that racial identity is not completely distinct from stage representation. To return to Twain's description of the minstrel show as a: "happy and accurate imitation of the usual and familiar negro quarrel", we can see that theatre's claims to accurate imitation are fraught and contested. Theatre can never be accurate or authentic: fundamentally, images onstage are intensely artificial embodiments of fantasies. However, *claims* to authenticity at the theatre have immense power, in the ways that they posit a direct relationship between the identity represented on the stage and the identity lived in the auditorium or in the street. Claims to the authentic have formative effects, producing attitudes and experiences of identity. The theatre's relationship to the real world, therefore, is not in the least straightforward, and the study of black make-up in performance can show us that authenticity is a deeply murky term when it comes to the stage.

Of course, we might feel that this problem with authenticity can be rectified, by reversing the casting of black roles. If black actors take over the performance of blackness on the stage, surely they produce a much more truthful and "real" representation of racial identity? This was certainly the claim made when black actors began to play the role of Othello, perhaps the most famous black stage role. However, the complexities of claims to authenticity do not necessarily recede when actors play people like them. The residues of minstrelsy have continued to show on the twentieth century stage.

Othello and the Residue of Minstrelsy

When the African American actor Paul Robeson tackled the role of Othello in London in 1930, he was imagined to be naturally capable of playing the character. Another black actor, Earle Hyman, said of his performance: 'he did not have to act' (cited in Potter, 2002, p. 132). In the reception of Robeson's performance, the trans-historical figure of Othello fixed black identity in its diverse socio-political and national forms, coming to stand in for all black identity everywhere. The idea that Robeson was 'naturally' suited to the role suggested that the characteristics Othello embodies are innate to blackness. The reception of Robeson's performance suggests that the idea of authenticity in performance is not only problematic when it describes white actors in blackface. Assumptions about the fixity of black identity have often informed descriptions of black actors onstage too.

Paul Robeson's performance was reported in reviews as: 'vivid acting as the terrible Moor. Kissing Scene. Coloured audience in the stalls' (cited in Potter, 2002, p. 119). The white critics were scandalised by a "real" black actor kissing the white actress Peggy Ashcroft, who played Desdemona. This kiss was a simultaneous interruption and repetition of the play's fictional narrative, in which Desdemona's father is also scandalised by the Moor Othello kissing his daughter. Just as the act of kissing onstage disrupted and reinforced the illusion of the fictional kiss, so too, the figure of Paul Robeson was meshed with that of Othello in the reception of the performance, suggesting that black identity was defined by a set of atavistic qualities such as wild passion, jealousy, violence and gullibility. The fact that Robeson was a lawyer who was forced to turn to acting because of discrimination against blacks in the legal profession did not mitigate against the idea that his blackness had inherent qualities that meant that 'he did not have to act'. The "authenticity" that critics and fellow actors saw in Robeson's performance was actually a product of the character he played.

A performance history of *Othello* suggests that roles can be stained by make-up: that characters may still bear the traces of burnt cork imprinted in their hairline or behind their ears, traces that transfer symbolically onto the appearance of the black actors who play them. Representations of blackness onstage do not necessarily escape associations with minstrelsy, even if they are embodied by black actors. Audiences may still imprint actors with the imaginary residues of the minstrel stage. Just as minstrelsy is an act of dressing-down, a shift in status that is at the heart of its racist pleasures for a white audience, here, the history of a stage-role may also become a dressing-down for the actor who embodies it, where the actor's appearance is formed and framed by the legacies of the character's previous stage-life.

As a result of the role's tendency to "fix" black performers, the post-civil rights critique of blackface has approached Othello with two main strategies. The first has been to cast black actors in the part, re-imagining and reformulating the role. The second has been to cast white actors without black make-up, depoliticising the performance by suggesting that the role, situation and character of Othello is "universal", and unattached to racial identity. For example, Jonathan Miller cast Anthony Hopkins in the role in 1981, arguing that: 'casting a black actor would equate the supposed simplicity of the black with the exorbitant jealousy of the character' (cited in Potter, 2002, p. 154). Miller argued that he wanted to explore the universal of qualities of jealousy and rage, universal qualities that were now represented in the white body of Hopkins.

Of course, there is a third strategy for the performance of Othello, which was suggested by the British black actor, Hugh Quarshi in a speech at the University of Alabama:

> when a black actor plays a role written for a white actor in black make-up and for a predominantly white audience, does he not encourage the white way, or rather the wrong way, of looking at black men, namely that black men, or "Moors", are over emotional, excitable and unstable, thereby vindicating Iago's statement, "these Moors are changeable in their wills"? Of all the parts in the canon, perhaps Othello is the one which should most definitely not be played by a black actor.
>
> (cited in Potter, 2002, p. 169)

Quarshi suggests that *not* playing the role should be a strategy for black performers, seeing Othello as too visibly imprinted by the blackface tradition. For Quarshi, actors should foreground the role as a white vision of blackness, and this should be achieved by casting a white actor. Quarshi's approach is echoed by the Nigerian playwright, S. E. Ogude, who argued:

> A black Othello is an obscenity. The element of the grotesque is best achieved when a white man plays the role. As the play wears on, and under the heat of lights and action, the make-up begins to wear off, Othello becomes a monstrosity of colours: the wine-red lips and snow white eyes again a background of messy blackness.
>
> (cited in Potter, 2002, p. 175)

For Ogude, the slippage of the make-up reveals the grotesque racist mask constructed by blackface. As with Quarshi, Ogude favours foregrounding the play's performance history, by acknowledging that for hundreds of years *only* white actors could play the role. Both of these critiques emphasise the formative effects of performance history on the body of a character, suggesting that stage roles cannot be completely distinguished from the many actors that have played them. The ghostly effects of accumulated past performances will be examined in Chapter 6, but what is crucial for my argument now is how Quarshi and Ogude both acknowledge the broader political context of theatrical legacies on the identity and reception of the black actor in performance.

The formative effects of the legacies of minstrelsy on black actors are also the central theme of Ntozake Shange's play *spell no 7*, written in 1979. On the stage from the beginning of the play hangs an enormous minstrel mask, which dominates the subsequent performance (see Shange, 1991, p. 71).

The mask has a similar effect to Ogude's vision of melting make-up, establishing a Brechtian disruption of the audience's ability to project authenticity onto the performers, forcing them to confront how the meanings of the mask visually and psychically dominate the experiences of the African American characters. Shange's characters appear onstage in minstrel masks, and move through a history of black entertainment in the United States, visibly formed by the legacies of that history. Shange implicates theatrical representation itself in the mediation and repression of the African American experience, staging the formative effects of the minstrel stage on lived black experience and establishing a discomfiting tension between the minstrel mask's grotesque gaping smile, and the traumatised bodies of the black characters who struggle to survive beneath its gaze.

Shange, Quarshi and Ogunde argue for the political necessity of making the distinction between actors and their roles visible. They all insist on an acknowledgement of the formative effects of the performance histories of roles: recognising that an actor can never perform a character without being situated within its legacies. The relationship between the real and the illusion is therefore inherently concerned with power: the power of a character to stand in for an entire race, the power to form identities by performing them and the power of some social groups to represent others. The idea of authenticity is fundamentally problematised by these artists, and they suggest that authenticity is a fantasy of a performance rather than something established in advance of it. Demonstrating that an actor is not who they play is a central tool for the critique of white versions of blackness on the American and European stages. This approach took centre stage in 1993, when The Wooster Group pondered the histories and legacies of blackface in a production of *The Emperor Jones*.

The Emperor Jones

In the Wooster Group's production of Eugene O'Neill's play *The Emperor Jones*, the actor Willem Dafoe played two characters: Smithers, a white Cockney trader, and Lem the black chief of a Caribbean island. In order to play the roles, Dafoe's face appeared on a small TV monitor that was positioned centre stage. When he played Lem, his face was shown on the screen as a negative image (black with a white mouth), and when he played Smithers, the TV switched to a positive image (white faced with a black mouth). Dafoe's face was imprinted by televisual masks, which made the representation of race evidently theatrical. The colour-coding of the two characters was complicated further by the fact that Dafoe appeared onstage with his face painted white, dressed in black and white Japanese-style robes. In this production it was evident that Dafoe was not who he played.

What was peculiar about this scene though, was that there was no clear point of origin for the colour of either of his characters. Because Dafoe was painted white onstage, and his image was then turned black on TV, it was hard to say from which direction he was crossing. His white make-up was evidently artificial, and it was this whiteness that was reversed to the black image of Lem. His performance made it very clear that the actor was not the character, but at the same time it also made it difficult to distinguish between the real actor and the illusion of the roles that he played. The idea of authenticity was not so much critiqued in Dafoe's performance, as entirely eradicated by his televisual masks.

That the Wooster Group would use technology to construct an endlessly receding unstable image of identity is not particularly surprising. Formed in the late 1970s, the company has established itself at the vanguard of post-modern theatre experiment in New York's downtown theatre scene, and its work has often unsettled the stable points of the character/actor continuum that Shange and Quarshi also seek to disrupt. What is particularly notable in this instance however is that the company used white make-up in their staging of a play that in 1920 was heralded as an important landmark for the representation of race on the American stage. *The Emperor Jones* was the first Broadway production to feature a black actor in a lead role onstage. The play, which tells the story of Brutus Jones an African American Pullman Porter who escapes from a chain gang and becomes the emperor of a Caribbean Island, was hailed as a masterpiece for its expressionist investigation into the complexities of race and identity. O'Neill, a white Irish-American playwright did a radical thing: he not only wrote a play featuring a central black character, he also insisted on casting a black actor to play the role, challenging the orthodoxies of the minstrel stage by doing so. However, by the time the Wooster Group performed the play in 1993, the lead black role was played in blackface by the white actress Kate Valk, and the role of Smithers was played by Dafoe in whiteface. What's even more startling is that reviews of the performance claimed that, by using blackface, the company had found a way to circumvent the racist portrayal of the central black protagonist.

How might this be? Why would a play that in 1920 was hailed by white audiences for its accuracy, for its genuinely authentic portrayal of blackness, now require minstrel techniques to relieve it of its racism? O'Neill's play seemed to promise the alternative to minstrelsy by writing a play for a real black actor. However, like Othello, the black actor who played the role was fixed by the look of the audience: his body was made an erotic and exotic spectacle in performance. While O'Neill consciously sought to resist the repressive attitudes towards blackness in his play, he nonetheless reaffirmed many of the stereotypes of blackness by confining black identity to the authentic and primitive "black body", a body performed by African-American actors such as Charles Gilpin and Paul Robeson. The Wooster Group's performance did not so much reverse the play's tendencies, as stage the confusions at the heart of the play's attitude to racial identity. We can see in *The Emperor Jones* the claims that Quarshi and Shange make about the legacies of minstrelsy for black performers: the ways in which the image of blackness produced by minstrelsy may infect black actors, even when the production makes a very conscious attempt to reject its legacies.

Indeed, the rejection of minstrelsy is at the heart of O'Neill's characterisation of the play's lead, Brutus Jones. Notably, however, in order to reject minstrelsy, O'Neill employs another form of cross-dressing: "whiting-up". When Jones enters the stage, it is his appearance that O'Neill first describes. Jones wears: 'a light blue uniform coat, sprayed with brass buttons, [. . .] his pants are bright red with a light blue stripe down the side. Patent leather laced boots with brass spurs, and a belt with a long-barreled, pearl-handled revolver in a holster complete his make-up' (O'Neill, 1998, p. 116). This is an outfit that O'Neill describes as: 'not altogether ridiculous' (O'Neill, 1998, p. 116). Jones wears a version of a Western military uniform, an outfit that a leader of a country might wear. However, its garish colours, and its over-use of brass buttons exaggerate its contours, an effect similar the minstrel costume's satire of high fashion. Jones's costume exaggerates the power it is supposed to represent, although O'Neill does not allow Jones to appear completely ridiculous: he resists turning Jones into a minstrel clown. Instead, Jones is "not altogether" ridiculous: his dress might appear similar to the minstrel's, but there is something serious or powerful about him that prevents him from appearing a complete parody. Perhaps this "not altogether" aspect of Jones is due to the power relations between his body and the clothes: the audience is confronted with the menace of a black man dressing "up" in the garb of whiteness, an inverse effect to that of blackface minstrelsy, which relied on the comedy of white performers dressing "down" as black for the entertainment of its white audiences.

O'Neill's impulse to complicate the minstrel image – the desire to place Jones in a "not altogether" relation to the minstrel version of blackness – can also be seen in his description of Jones's face. Jones is: 'a tall, powerfully built, full-blooded Negro of middle age. His features are typically Negroid, yet there is something decidedly distinctive about his face' (O'Neill, 1998, p. 116). Unlike the minstrel make-up, which fixed and generalised the appearance of blackness, here O'Neill locates a distinctiveness in Jones that is again located in Jones's status as a leader, rather than a slave. However, O'Neill again supposes that the minstrel view of blackness is the norm, that "all black people look the same," and Jones is situated as an exception to a rule that emerged from the theatrical traditional that O'Neill sought to overthrow. Jones is established as a black man who masquerades as white through his exaggerated costume, which lends him a distinctiveness that hinges on power.

We can also see this relationship between race and power in the negotiations between Jones and Smithers, a white cockney trader, at the beginning of the play. Their relationship is underscored by their uneasy relations of power, with Jones's superior political power operating in conflict with Smithers' presumption of power through his whiteness. By placing these men in an antagonistic relationship, O'Neill suggests that racial relations are established through status, rather than through any innate qualities attached to the colour of skin. Indeed, the play emphasises Jones's impersonation of whiteness, telling Smithers:

> For de little stealin' dey gits you in jail soon or late. For de big stealin' dey makes you Emperor and puts you in de Hall O' Fame when you croaks. (Reminiscently) If dey's one thing I learns in ten years on de Pullman ca's listenin' to de white quality talk, it's dat same fact. And when I gits a chance to use it I winds up Emperor in two years.
>
> (O'Neill, 1998, p. 119)

Jones plays white by acting the tyrant. By emulating and imitating the "white quality" that he overheard when working on the Pullman railway, Jones has become as brutal a coloniser as he was once colonised. Jones achieves a highly successful performance of whiteness, asserted through behaviour that is centred on domination and exploitation. To act brutally and to construct an empire is to cross-dress as a white person, and Jones has learnt to mask himself as white through the economic exploitation of others, controlling the natives whom he contemptuously describes as 'ignorant bush niggers' (O'Neill, 1998, p. 118).

On discovering that the natives have mutinied, Jones retreats from his white palace to the darkness of the forest in a bid to escape on a ship, with all his misbegotten loot stored in a Swiss bank account. Losing his way through the forest, he hallucinates a series of scenes from his past. Jones's journey through the forest is a journey through his history. He is visited by visions of his time on a prison chain gang and of his murder of a man over a card game. Jones's unconscious past comes back to haunt him, driving him mad, and he is cast back even further, into visions of the history of his race, hallucinating a slave auction, a slave ship and finally his "primordial" roots in Africa, where he is confronted by a vision of a crocodile and a masked witch doctor. Jones is finally killed by the natives, and his dead body is displayed onstage at the end of the play.

The journey into history is mimicked by the journey of Jones's costume. He loses items of clothing as he goes, and his body becomes progressively more and more naked throughout his journey. By the end of the play: 'his pants have been so torn away that what is left of them is not better than a breech-cloth' (O'Neill, 1998, p. 145). As Jones's black skin becomes more visible, his behaviour becomes less powerful, becoming disoriented, abject, terrified and pleading. Historical and psychic regression in this play takes the form of a kind of striptease. Moving from the white space of civilisation, to the black space of the forest, Jones's white mask is stripped away to reveal the "authentic" identity beneath: embodied, superstitious, irrational and black. In a similar and inverse move from the minstrel performer establishing their white skin as a guarantor of the "real" body beneath their make-up, Jones's skin operates as the true and stable indicator of his "real" identity beneath his impersonation of whiteness. Like Othello's atavistic effects on the black performer, Jones is entrapped by a racial destiny that he cannot evade.

The play's journey into the history of Jones's race spells out a central contradiction in O'Neill's approach to colour. O'Neill challenged fixed racial hierarchies by demonstrating that race was formed through power rather than nature, by critiquing white identity as exploitative, and by historicising black identity in Jones's journey through racial history. However, he nonetheless simultaneously rendered race a stable, inescapable and corporeal fact. Jones's denial of his race leads to his death, and his body is asserted as the guarantor of the authenticity of his blackness. The play both deconstructs the static hierarchies of race which were prevalent at the time that O'Neill wrote his play, and simultaneously reaffirms them by showing Jones's racial cross-dressing to be unperformative: no matter how much Jones *acts* like a white man, he will never quite *be* a white man, and his black body is defenceless against the superstition of the natives and the atavistic claims of his race.

The manifold contradictions in the *Emperor Jones'* treatment of race were amplified in its 1920 performance. By leaning heavily on the idea of authenticity, the decision *not* to cast a blackened white actor in the role was haunted by minstrelsy. The production displayed the black body of the actor to its white audience as an object of desire, pleasure and revulsion. We could even argue that the black actors playing Jones were cross-dressing, or in blackface, when playing the role of Jones. Actors such as Charles

Gilpin, who played Jones in the first performance, were forced to embody an exaggerated blackness and to reveal their "authentic" black bodies on the stage. We might say that these actors were "passing" as black in performance: appearing to be black, but in fact mimicking a racial position that was not their own, but was rather a version of blackness by a white author. By entering into a representational economy of race in which they had no authorial position, the actors playing Jones both imitated a blackness constructed by O'Neill and furthermore emphasised their own black corporeality as a sign of their authenticity for the erudition of a white audience (see Steen, 2000).

While O'Neill used the loss of clothing to assert Jones's "authentic" body, he also established, for the white audience, an erotic visual relationship with Jones's black body. Of course, the audience did not only see the body of the character; they also, and more powerfully, saw the "authentic" black body of the actor playing Jones, stripped down to a loincloth. For an audience unused to seeing black actors onstage, the spectacle of Gilpin's naked body was inevitably exotic and erotic. Indeed, the white reception of the first performance glowingly reported of Gilpin that: 'we watched him lazily and gloatingly uncoil his sinuosities in the first scene with the stupefied recoil with which we might have watched the same process in the nodes of a boa constrictor' (O. W. Firkins cited in Wainscott, 1988, p. 56). Despite O'Neill's radical departure from the minstrel tradition, white critics were still putting the jungle into blackness, a response that contrasted sharply with the heckling from the African American audience at the Harlem revival who bade Jones to: 'come on out o' that jungle – back to Harlem where you belong!' (cited in Steen, 2000, p. 345). While Gilpin may have taken a crucial step in re-establishing African-American control over the representation of the black body onstage, he nonetheless had no authorial control over the actions of the character he played or over the white audience's visual relationship to his body.

By the time the Wooster Group came to perform *The Emperor Jones*, the play's unconscious influence by minstrelsy meant that it was now considered almost unstageable, as Jonathan Kalb argued: 'here is a classic play that is virtually unperformable in 1990s America in the manner the author envisioned in 1920. [...] Unfortunately, performed today as written (that is with earnest and realistic emotion by a black actor), the cunning yet superstitious and uneducated Jones too easily comes off as a racist stereotype' (Kalb, 1998, p. 6). Indeed, we could read the use of blackface and whiteface in the Wooster Group's production of *The Emperor Jones* as a straightforward critique of O'Neill's idea of authentic blackness. Kate Valk, in the lead role, not only wore blackface, she also impersonated and exaggerated minstrel vocal patterns. Meanwhile, Dafoe's Smithers was a stylized and feminised ghostly figure that haunted Jones throughout the journey in the forest through the TV monitors and microphones. The production's exaggerated use of colour foregrounded the unconscious influence of minstrelsy on O'Neill's representation of the "authentic" black body. The distinction between actor and role was absolutely crucial for this effect: the use of make-up did not so much represent character, as comment on it. And the commentary was not only on the character, but also on the theatrical legacies, and performance histories of that character. The company did not just perform the play, they also enacted and deconstructed its performance history.

However, the production did something even more complicated than critique O'Neill's "authentic" representations of blackness. As we saw in the instance of Dafoe on the TV monitor, the use of black and white make-up also succeeded in unsettling the relationship between the actor and the role, making the distinction between the real and the illusion difficult to establish. Because Dafoe's whiteface did not evoke a racial whiteness but a theatrical one, the production suggested that blackface was also a theatrical mask, having little to do with "real" blackness. Furthermore, while Kate Valk's face was painted black, her neck was painted red, and her arms and feet were left unpainted, making it very clear that this was make-up, not skin. Unlike the minstrel make-up, which claimed to be authentic (while declaring at the same time that the performer was "not black"), here the make-up was clearly fake, making *whiteness*, as well as blackness, strange onstage, constantly reminding the audience that the actors' coloured faces were theatrical rather than biological constructs.

Additionally, for an audience familiar with the play, the expectation of the striptease in the forest was thwarted. Like a Russian doll, Jones's undressing did not reveal a real body, but simply displayed further layers of costuming. As the character lost his clothes, Valk's costume lost its Japanese qualities and revealed an American-style plaid shirt and an African print skirt underneath the Kabuki style robes. Furthermore, the loss of the robes revealed Valk's arms which were left unpainted, making her blackface all the more theatrical. In the original production, the peeling away of the layers of Jones's clothing revealed the authenticity of Charles Gilpin's black body beneath the clothes. In the Wooster Group's staging of this striptease, the layers of clothing were themselves significant of different kinds of bodies: racial, cultural, gendered and historical. From Japanese to (literally) African/American clothing, from blackened features to white arms and feet, Valk's Jones did not unearth an authentic body beneath the costume, but revealed another set of representations beneath the layer of aristocratic,

Orientalist, blackface masculinity, implying that her body was produced *through* costume.

The Wooster Group's use of make-up suggested that Brutus Jones was a purely theatrical invention, an invention mediated through minstrelsy, with consequences for how audiences and performers might embody race after the performance ended. The Wooster Group's treatment of race-as-mask, suggested that there was no true body beneath the make-up: that masks *are* identity, rather than concealing a true self "underneath" the fiction. Here, therefore, the make-up doesn't conceal identity, rather it invents it: identity is fundamentally theatrical. Unlike Eugene O'Neill's play, in which the masking of the self is punished by history, and the colour of the body is the guarantor of the authentic self, the Wooster Group suggested that the "real" body is made *through* its masking, that in fact, the mask *constitutes* the real. The act of impersonation was imagined as not just something actors do, therefore: crossing was positioned as a broader social act that produces the body, an effect that Judith Butler terms "performativity" (see Butler, 1999, p. 171). The "authentic" body was clearly a product of performance, and the spectator became uncomfortably complicit with the absence, presence and materialisation of race in the Wooster Group's work. While Eugene O'Neill posited the act of crossing as a form of deception that ultimately leads to death, the Wooster Group framed crossing as an inevitable mode of materialising identity. While O'Neill rejected cross-dressing as a viable mode of identity, the Wooster Group showed crossing and theatricality to be an inescapable tragedy.

True and Natural Bodies

Returning to *Shakespeare in Love*, we can see that the question posed by Judi Dench as Queen Elizabeth I, 'can a play show us the very truth and nature of love?' (Norman and Stoppard, 1999, p. 95), is a useful one for our investigation into the effects that costume can have on identity. When actors cross over the borders of identity, their act of crossing can question the very concepts of "truth" and "nature". Theatre invokes and invents bodies through the act of crossing, and changing clothes can mean changing bodies on the stage and in the audience. Cross-dressing allows us to see the connection between costumed performance, and the concept of "performativity": the ability of performance not just to imitate, but also to invent and perpetuate further ways of doing the body. To tamper with the categories of clothing and make-up is to remake bodies and identities. Imagine, then, that the boy player's costume in *Shakespeare in Love*, actually transforms the way in which he is gendered, sexualised or ranked. Imagine that

Joseph Murphy's cross-dressing is not only a performance, but performative, with the black make-up and woman's dress having a material effect on his body. Imagine also, that the audience watching his performance are in some way themselves reconfigured by the act of mutual consent to suspend disbelief, and believe that the actor is not only "a woman", but a "black American woman". Imagine that our own faces are like Dafoe's receding masks, formed through performance without a single point of origin.

Theatre often relies heavily on the idea of a stable point of origin for the logic of acting. Minstrel performers blacked up in order to point to their whiteness beneath their make-up. White audiences watched black performers play Othello, and imagined that the performance was governed by a set of fixed characteristics that defined the character and the actor simultaneously. However, as we have seen in both cases, this point of origin is a fantasy of the performance rather than something established in advance of it. Fundamentally, the performance of the real onstage is an intensely artificial act. Nonetheless, *claims* to the real are very powerful, and those claims may have crucial effects on the absent identity embodied by actors, and on the identity of the actors themselves. By going to the theatre, we are all bellowing that "that woman is a woman" but not always with comic effect.

5
Undressing: The Disappointments of Nudity

In 2007, the actor Daniel Radcliffe (of *Harry Potter* fame) starred in a production of *Equus* in London's West End. The play is known for its requirement of full frontal nudity from its lead actor, and the production garnered huge press attention even before it opened. This, the pre-publicity promised, was the performance in which we would see Harry Potter naked. The theatre reviewers from the *West End Whingers* blog describe the moment when Radcliffe undressed onstage, and its effect on the audience:

> And *that* scene? You have to wait until the last 15 minutes of the play for it. [...] 900 pairs of eyes concentrated on one small area of the stage. [...] As he dropped his drawers the focus of the play became very different indeed. However sophisticated and mature the audience believe themselves to be this was the big (or perhaps not) moment. All coughing stopped as one special cast member took the spotlight. The Whingers are far too polite to comment further (unlike others), but, as one couple cruelly remarked leaving the Gielgud, "You'd need binoculars for that one".
>
> (2007, p. 1)

The Whingers' characteristically witty review is revealing of the broader effects of nudity onstage. Here, we have a theatrical moment, "*that* scene", the moment of undressing that is somehow distinct from all the others in the performance. This moment is of course the revelation of the penis. Somehow, the act of undressing produces a shift in focus (the audience even stop coughing), where the act of *looking* becomes pronounced – necessitating the cruel remark about binoculars. We have already seen binoculars at the theatre in Renoir's painting in Chapter 2, but they are no longer required for viewing other audience members. Now binoculars are specifically for viewing penises onstage.

Why might this be? Why would the genitals of an actor, specifically a film star, command such rapt attention? Perhaps we need to consider this moment as centred less on the exposure of genitals, and more on the theatrical act of undressing onstage. It's worth considering whether Radcliffe would have had such an impact if he had appeared naked from the beginning of the show. It seems to me, that the sense of "event" or "scene" is made possible by him "dropping his drawers": the drama of the revelation of his genitals would not have been so great if he had no clothes to take off to begin with. It is the presence of clothes in the act of undressing, rather than their absence, that makes his nudity spectacular. And it is in this act of divesting that the presence of the film star *himself* becomes available: "now", the undressing seems to promise, 'now, we will see Harry Potter ... or, Daniel Radcliffe ... *as he really is* before us onstage.' The secrets of the real actor that the dressing room portraits promise and fail to betray are also built into the promise of nudity. Somehow, we will access the actor in all his vulnerable privacies. Somehow, nudity will allow us to see the truth. Somehow we will see what the actor looked like all along *beneath* his costume. It is no accident that this revelation of truth comes 15 minutes before the end of the show: just as the crime is solved, or the romantic errors of comedy are ironed out at the end of the drama, so too, the actor is finally revealed with the promise of truth and insight. Harry Potter appears naked before our very eyes.

Nudity might be imagined as the great exception to the premise of this book. I've argued so far that costume is what makes the actor possible on the stage, but naked actors seem to contradict this argument. After all, we can see actors onstage without any costume on at all. And certainly, as in the case of Daniel Radcliffe, their nakedness makes actors seem even more present, even more available *as* actors to the greedy eyes of the spectator. Surely, nudity disproves the idea that the actor is inherently costumed? Perhaps. However, it is with the very peculiar effect that nudity has on presence that this chapter concerns itself, and I'm not convinced that this effect isn't centred entirely on costume. In fact, I'm going to argue throughout this chapter, that clothing is at the centre of the effects of nudity: nudity is a form of costume and couldn't take place without it. Furthermore, I'm going to suggest that nudity onstage is often achieved through the visible and theatrical act of undressing, and that it is undressing rather than nudity that produces this effect on the actor's presence.

The performer's presence seems to magnify when naked, becoming extra-present in performance, and this presence is often felt to disrupt the field of the narrative illusion. The nude body appears stubbornly resistant to its inclusion in the fiction, just as, as phenomenologists have suggested, dogs and children are (see States, 1985, p. 32). The naked body certainly stands in for other people and qualities, but it also "just is" onstage: providing a blunt kind of realism that complicates the actor's role in the world of illusion. As Karl Toepfer argues: 'theatrical nudity awakens complicated "problems" concerning the "reality" of the performing body' (Toepfer, 1996, p. 76). Ironically, perhaps, the only time that this effect does not seem to take place is in striptease, where the act of disrobing is so conventionalised that the performer recedes beneath the weight of ritualised codes of nakedness. In other forms of nude performance though, like celebrity nudity or avant-garde theatre or performance art, the nude performer stands out, disrupting the frame, becoming more than themselves once their bodies are bared.

However, while the naked body appears to gain in distinctiveness from the illusion on the stage, I want to suggest in this chapter that it is in the intermediary act of undressing that these peculiarities of nudity are revealed. It is not in the body's bare state that the presence of the performer is so asserted: rather it is in the body's revelations through the additions and removals of clothing that this effect on presence is possible. However, if we look closely at undressing we can see that the body is not revealed, in some sort of truthful state beneath the clothing, but is rather reformed and remade by the act of undressing. When we watch the actor undressing, we see a series of bodies emerging, which are determined by their relation to clothes. In this, the naked body seems peculiar and stubbornly present because of its uncanniness: it doesn't look like it should, or rather it doesn't look the way the clothes made it look, and yet it still bears traces of the clothes it once wore. Undressing doesn't betray the secret of what is beneath the costume; it simply establishes more secrets and more costumes. Like the Russian Doll effect of Kate Valk peeling off her clothes in *The Emperor Jones*, so too the revelation of the naked body simply reveals further costumes: the costume of nakedness, the costume of skin or the costume of the traditions of the nude female figure. We can't access this seemingly brutally real body *as* real: its reality is an illusion, a fantasy. No mystery is revealed. Rather, new layers of costumes appear which might explain why nudity is often so terribly disappointing on the stage.

In thinking about this peculiar issue of presence, we need to raise some subsidiary questions concerning nudity's role within the conditions of performance, asking what nudity's effects are on: clothing, pleasure (of the spectator and perhaps the performer), theatricality, objects, speech and time. This chapter is centrally concerned with the role that undressing plays in establishing stage nakedness, in an attempt to get at the relationship nudity has with costume. Also of importance however, is the ways in which nudity offers us an insight into the relationship between looking and power in performance, allowing us to examine the erotic not as an incidental pleasure, but one central to the experience of theatricality. In this, the power of the spectator to look at performers, the spectator's occasional slide into the role of the voyeur, and the ways that nude performance can reward or punish the Peeping Tom role, are all key to a consideration of nudity onstage. The chapter will examine four kinds of nakedness onstage: striptease, male nakedness, celebrity undressing and post-modern undress in order to consider the disappointments of nudity.

Striptease

In the early twentieth century in New York, a favoured striptease act was one in which a scantily clad dancer put her clothes on onstage. Dressing-up was an inverse act of stripping that offered similar pleasures to the performances of undressing, as Brenda Foley argues: 'covering the exposed body in front of the audience was a variation of a common burlesque device used to situate the spectator as voyeur' (Foley, 2005, p. 46).Fundamentally, it didn't matter too much for the erotic dimensions of striptease which direction the clothing went, as long as clothes were being added or removed. The act of undressing, then, is crucial to the pleasures of striptease. Once the task of dressing or undressing makes the (female) performer appear absorbed in her task, the (male) spectator is free to look at her body voyeuristically. Furthermore, dressing or undressing establishes a "normal" body (naked or clothed) and taking off or putting on clothes then crosses the boundary of that normal body. It is less the loss of clothing that matters, as much as the shift in the boundaries of the body that makes the striptease erotic. Indeed, it is the performer's relationship with costume that produces the frisson of the striptease. After all, neither the naked, nor the clothed, body is particularly erotic – it is in the act of disrobing that both costume and body become erotically charged.

This example tells us a number of things about the relationship between clothing and striptease. Fundamentally, striptease is centred on the relationship between clothes and the anticipation of nudity. The act of undressing is governed by the fantasy of transgression, and the structures of convention, ritual and repetition in performance. It is the transgression of the body's appearance that is at the heart of the act: clothes are central to establishing borders of the body, which can then be crossed. However, the strip artist does not baldly take off her clothes. Rather, she takes off (or puts on) her clothes in theatrically conventional ways, employing a dance style, a set of costumes, music and a particular spatial relationship between spectator and performer to do so. It is exactly through these conventions, rituals and boundaries that nakedness is made impossible by striptease. The body of the performer is rendered so codified that it is not possible to see nakedness in any real way: rather the spectator sees artifice, and indeed, the performance generally ends once all the clothes are gone, making the process of undressing far more important than the bare body it supposedly reveals.

Given that striptease relies on the act of undressing, a number of scholars have argued that objective nakedness is made impossible in art and theatre. Contrary to a feminist reading of bodily objectification as dehumanising, Roland Barthes sees in the ritual tendency of striptease performance a version of costume, arguing of strip artists: 'their science clothes them like a garment' (Barthes, 1982, p. 87). Barthes points to the ways in which the female stripper's body is made aesthetic through the codified uses of costume: 'the furs, the fans, the gloves, the feathers, the fish-net stockings, in short, the whole spectrum of adornment, constantly makes the living body return to the category of objects which surround man with a luxurious magical décor' (Barthes, 1982, p. 86). The conventions of costume render the stripper's body a ritual object. Furthermore, the familiar repetitive nature of the dance, "clothes" the body with form. The dance: 'acts on movements as a cosmetic, it hides real nudity, and smothers the spectacle under a gaze of superfluous yet essential gestures' (Barthes, 1982, p. 87). Undressing is at the heart of striptease and is, at the same time, a means to guarantee that the body never really appears naked: it is always protected by the object-hood gained through its costume.

Barthes' discussion of striptease is a typically provocative and witty semiotics of nudity. His argument is problematic, in its presumption of a male reader and an uncomplicated objectified female body, and in its somewhat simplistic notion of a "real nudity" by contrast with the staged one of striptease. However, his essay is helpful in acknowledging how dancers undressing in performance continue to be costumed through the use of repetition and convention. Barthes suggests that nudity is another kind of costume onstage, that the naked body is hidden by the conventions of nudity in performance. Indeed, the impossibility of actual nakedness has also been discussed by the art historian Anne Hollander, who argues that clothing is the framework through which the body is imagined, meaning that nakedness is the effect of clothing rather than something that exists in advance of it. As Hollander suggests, fashion moulds our idea of the body, so that when naked: 'people without clothes are still likely to behave as if they wore them' (Hollander, 1993, p. 87). The representations of the nude onstage and in paintings are moulded through clothing, and, as such, nudity is a form of costuming, with its own bodily decorum, conventions and regulations.

The suggestion that undressing is fundamentally an artificial and aesthetic act is echoed in art historian Kenneth Clark's distinction between the straightforward bareness of nakedness, and the nude: 'not [as] the subject of art, but a form of art' (Clark, 1956, p. 3). I'm sure Clark would have been horrified to find his views applied to the lowly form of striptease (Clark saw the nude as the ideal of high culture, not as the outcome of an art designed to titillate). However, his distinction is both useful and problematic for our discussion of undressing onstage. On the one hand, it's helpful to distinguish between a body that just happens to have no clothes on, and a body whose nudity is aestheticised by entering the realm visual art or performance. On the other hand, the notion that a body can ever "just" be naked, erroneously suggests that bodies can exist beyond the effects of representation. Indeed, Lynda Nead has argued that the tradition of the female nude in art has functioned as a patriarchal regulation of real women's bodies, disciplining their messy contours and reducing their subversive possibilities (see Nead, 1992, p. 7). Nead suggests that to elevate the nude above the naked is to see the male artist's aestheticised version of female bodies as far preferable to the bodies themselves. As a result, women's own bodies are judged according to an artistic tradition within which, until recently, they have had little stake or influence, except as the powerless figure of the muse (see Nead, 1992, p. 14).

However, this discussion makes little space for the act of undressing. Is the intermediate position of the undressing body more or less nude? After all, undressing in theatrical performance, rather than in visual art, presents the added complexity of bodies that *move*. When the undressing dancer moves, she risks exceeding her aesthetic containment as a nude body, and becoming worryingly naked. The possibility of accidents or mistakes in performance adds an even greater tension to the stakes involved in theatrical undressing. Indeed, there has been a long history of legislation and censorship surrounding the exposure of the naked body onstage that has centred on the opposition between movement and stasis. Fundamentally, the desire to control this opposition between movement and stasis is based on the desire to retain the body as an aesthetic object, and to prevent the appearance of the "real" in performance (see Foley, 2005, p. 19). To move while undressing risks a shift from a carefully contained and safely nude body to the messiness of the "real" naked body. Not only does this naked performer move: she might also speak, and speech potentially imbues the naked body with subjectivity. This may explain why many scenes involving undressing onstage are undertaken in silence.

In striptease, a form generally performed without speech, the opposition between the objectified passive (female) body displayed for voyeuristic (male) pleasure, and the active subjectivity of the moving female performer, is evident. The rituals and conventions attached to striptease that Barthes describes might be imagined as performative strategies of containment that regulate the body in equivalent ways to the stasis of the nude in painting. Barthes' list of the ritualised aspects of costume, movement and roles in striptease, signals the need to make the undressing female body safe. The environment of striptease, as Brenda Foley points out, operates as a series of visual and physical constraints: glass cages, catwalks and bars, alongside the constraining forces of convention: the repetitive dance, familiar costumes and codified gestures and expressions that Barthes outlines (see Foley, 2005, p. 20). These physical and gestural constraints work to contain the potential transgression of female nudity. Striptease therefore becomes a codified gesture of eroticism, rather than actually *being* erotic, just as the stripper's undressing body promises nudity, but is never quite naked.

Fundamentally, the erotic in striptease is made possible *through* these forms of containment, rather than despite them. The naked body in isolation has a much less powerfully erotic effect than one that interacts with dress, space and objects. Anne Hollander argues of the nude in paintings: 'the nude in a room with a cast-off pile of garments, particularly if accompanied by dressed attendants or observers, had always been an erotic theme, which also gained in intensity through the inclusion [...] of everyday objects' (Hollander, 1993, p. 175). The voyeuristic spectator cannot enjoy the nudity of the body unless it is surrounded by objects and clothing that emphasise its bareness. The purely naked body is self-contained and impermeable, whereas the nude body surrounded by objects, reaches out into the world, and destabilises its borders. Its nakedness becomes available to the gaze of the viewer via the objects that surround it. We need to see the body through things in order for its own thingliness to become available. And the central relationship with things in striptease is established in the performer's act of undressing, in her use of costume. Her body, in the act of undressing, can be imagined by the viewer as sensuous and tactile. The fantasy of the feeling of flesh against fabric is transmitted to the spectator, whose relationship to the stripping performer is not entirely ocular: it is also one of projected tactility. As Anne Hollander suggests: 'the sensuous pleasure taken by the hairless human body in the sliding touch of fabric is conjured by any image of draped flesh' (Hollander, 1993, p. 84).

In the end, clothing in striptease creates the body to be divested. Taking off clothes operates as a form of close-up, drawing attention to specific parts of the body, and dividing the body into different zones of meaning and eroticism. As a result, just as the dancer's body is clothed by ritual, her body is also fragmented by dress and undressing. Henry Jarrett announced in 1897 that: 'legs are staple articles and will never go out of business while the world lasts' (cited in Foley, 2005, p. 15). Legs, breasts, buttocks, arms, décolletage and genitals have been exposed and framed by the costume of striptease at varying moments in history, and this costume works to emphasise the areas that are to be denuded in the implied future of the performance. These close ups established through costume, establish the boundaries of the body which will then be transgressed by the act of undressing. These boundaries are often set up in advance of the performance by fashionable dress. The concealment of ankles and legs by the nineteenth-century female dress, for example, meant that legs were the central focus of burlesque and vaudeville revues in the late nineteenth century. Undressing, then, makes nudity a site-specific act, specific to the histories of fashion, art and the location of the erotic in the social boundaries of the body. Nudity is the outcome of clothes.

Looking and Power

The erotic is established by striptease because it ensures that the performer will be absorbed in the task of undressing. The spectator can watch the performer while the performer looks away (very like the portrait of the actress by Degas in Chapter 1). The theatricality of striptease reveals how theatre's investment in pleasure is inherently concerned with power, and shows us that the act of looking is not neutral. Indeed, Western culture is permeated by myths of nudity that centre on ways of seeing. The stories of Adam and Eve, The Emperor's New Clothes, and Lady Godiva all rely on a relationship between dressing and viewing for their central theme. Adam and Eve only become "naked" when God punishes them by making them look with shame at their own unclothed state. The Emperor's New Clothes is a satire on the shared agreement to "see" bodies as clothed through the (hypocritical) frameworks of power and hierarchy. Peeping Tom spies on Lady Godiva, who strips naked and rides her horse through Coventry in order to persuade her husband to reduce the crippling taxes on his people. The sight of her body blinds Tom, punishing him for his illicit voyeurism. These stories suggest that it is not nudity, but the relationship between undressing and looking that is of concern for Western representation. The stories ask: Is it nudity or clothing that is the more shameful? How is the act of looking at bodies rewarded or punished? Is it possible to see naked bodies without seeing clothes?

The power relations involved in the act of looking, and their implications for the representation and experience of gender identity, have been outlined in some detail by feminist scholars. Laura Mulvey's seminal 1975 essay, 'Visual Pleasure and Narrative Cinema', argued that: 'there are circumstances in which looking itself is a source of pleasure' (Mulvey, 1998, p. 270). Mulvey's work takes a psycho-analytic approach to the act of looking in cinema, and shows that films are often constructed so that the "male gaze" is privileged within the narrative and within the audience. Male spectators can enjoy looking at women in the scene of a film, and can project themselves in identification with the male protagonists who also look at women within the scene. On the other hand, the woman in the film is positioned as an object of that gaze, existing to be looked at: 'women are simultaneously looked at and displayed, with their appearance coded for strong visual and erotic impact so that they can be said to connote *to-be-looked-at-ness*' (Mulvey, 1998, p. 272). The fact that women exist in film as objects to be looked at, means that the female spectator is placed in an ambiguous and problematic position when viewing the film. As Jill Dolan argues: 'she cannot find a comfortable way into the representation, since she finds herself, as a woman [...] excluded from its address' (Dolan, 1998, p. 289). Mulvey and Dolan both examine how the structures of narrative in film and theatre simultaneously exclude the female spectator, and objectify the female performer.

The theory of the male gaze has been revised extensively (particularly by Mulvey), and theatre scholars have also problematised the application of film theory to the very different form of looking that theatre entails. Nonetheless, the principle that the act of looking is not a neutral act, but is inherently constructed through power relations, and has a material effect on how gender is represented, continues to influence feminist thought. While the nudity of the female stripper might be protected by the ritual elements of their performance, nonetheless, the performance is constructed so that the male spectator can watch – their own bodies and identities untouched by the performance – while the female performer dances. Furthermore, this theory of looking shows that it is necessary for the dancer to be turned into an object, in order for the pleasure in looking on the spectator's part to be possible. It is essential that the dancer's body is contained within the boundaries established by the rituals of dance and space, and the absorption in the act of undressing, so that the viewer can gaze with impunity, never confronted by dancer as a subject. We can see then, that undressing is centrally concerned with establishing boundaries of the body in order to establish the pleasures of looking, which are centred on the viewer having far more power than the viewed.

In the end, stage nudity shows us how much costuming is embroiled in relations of power: indeed, how costuming is the outcome of power. We saw in the last chapter how cross-dressing negotiates between the status of the performer and the status of the figure that the performer represents. In striptease, costume reconfigures the status of actors so that they become objects to be looked at. This approach shares similarities with the view of actors held by Edward Gordon Craig in Chapter 3, and the Duke of Monmouth's approach to Mr Noaks in Chapter 2. Perhaps then, the objectification of actors through undressing is not so much a special case, than an exemplification of the broader complexity of looking at actors at the theatre. The objectification of undressing actors is certainly gendered in this case, but it may also be indicative of a wider dynamic of the erotics of looking at the theatre.

Male Nudity

In July 2005, British journalists reported that Tony Blair, England's then prime minister, had spent £1800 over six years on cosmetics, including fake tan. The news hit during a silly season lull after the 7/7 London bombings, and media pundits rushed to deliver their verdict on the story. A Conservative spokesperson argued that: 'this just goes to show how cosmetic this government has become' (cited in Hinsliff, 2005, p. 19), while the *Sunday Times* suggested that Blair's expenditure on make-up had radically increased during his defence of the use of inaccurate intelligence reports on weapons of mass destruction in Iraq (Govan, 2005, p. 16). Journalists interpreted Blair's fake tan as a comic sign of his inner falsehood, and their commentary suggested that Blair's outer appearance was expressive of his inner being. The use of make-up was viewed as a form of trickery by these reports, suggesting that altering one's appearance is a kind of lying. Furthermore, the media debate implied that Blair could have presented his body in a way that was *not* adorned, embellished or "made-up". The idea of a body that could be honest and unadorned was produced by default in the coverage of this story. However, we might question whether this "honest" body is in any way possible. Even without his make-up, Blair inevitably and automatically constructed his body for the public gaze. The notion of an "honest" body relies on the idea that costume and make-up are dishonest, and that an alternative is possible.

Modifying the male body is often seen as both false and funny. The laughter at Blair's expenditure on make-up is echoed in the Whingers' tongue in cheek description of Daniel Radcliffe's nudity in *Equus*. Why might this be?

Why would the modification of male appearance draw laughter or mockery rather than offering voyeuristic pleasure? Why would female nudity be considered erotic and male nudity funny? Perhaps modifying the body, or undressing, is read as a kind of dressing down? In order for the balance of power to be on the spectator's side the audience situates the performer's naked body as an object, rendering the performer a thing to be looked at. We have seen that this power shift is necessary for establishing an erotic dimension to looking at female performers. This may be why the idea of naked men may not be so erotic – their drop in power, which is less usual in the traditions of representing men, might be viewed as disturbing rather than sexy. As we saw in the case of Joseph Murphy, a performer "dressing down" can be seen as a form of mockery or comedy in male performance. Similarly, Blair's body, and character, is read as weak and unstable by his need to change his appearance. Clothes, then, are crucial for masculinity's status, a status that is undermined by the loss of those clothes when men undress onstage.

The fact that undressing is a way for performers to lose their status, may explain why the male body is often presented in an already-undressed state onstage in performance art. For a performance artist to appear onstage naked, male and not be funny seems to require that nudity be established from the get-go, rather than emerging from the act of undressing. Naked male bodies are a commonplace of body and performance art; forms that emerged from the visual art and avant-garde practices of the early twentieth century. In order to ensure that the realness and presence of the male body is paramount, without comic effect, these performances have developed theatrical strategies of ritual and containment that are structurally similar to those of striptease. The performance work by the visual artist Franko B is a good example. Franko B is an Italian artist, based in London who has been using his own body as a form of art since the mid-1990s. Franko featured in an episode on body art as part of the British television series *The Southbank Show* in 1998. The documentary featured excerpts of his performance in an art gallery, which showed him naked (already undressed), in a pool of light, painted white. He poured a bag of his own blood over his head, so that the bloodstains were visible over the whiteness of his body, and held a bloodstained rag in his mouth. Buffeted by waves of dry ice, Franko bled from pumps that he had inserted into his arms. The blood created a pool on the floor, which he later lay in. His performance was witnessed by two figures in white coats and surgical masks who, at the end of the performance, tied his legs together with a rope and strung him upside down, hanging him from a meat hook. His body, white, bleeding and stained red from his own blood hung like a carcass in the circle of light.

The *Southbank* documentary interspersed these excerpts with scenes of Franko preparing for his performance, covering up his tattooed and pierced body with white make-up, which was applied by his assistants (the figures in the surgical masks). These assistants were dressers off the stage and medical controlling figures within the performance. (They were also shown helping to wash Franko B after the performance had ended.) The documentary relied on the allure of the dressing room, showing the actor in an intermediary state, preparing to perform. However, what was crucial for all of these preparations was Franko's insistence on the reality (rather than theatricality) of his performance. He emphasised the role of nudity in his performance as central to its truthfulness, as he explained to a journalist: 'I'm obsessed with presenting something in its purest state. [...] And if you're going to be naked you do it with honesty' (Halliburton, 2000, p. 5). Franko presented nudity as a form of honesty, in harmony with the reality of his own real-time bleeding onstage. Franko B's performance was dependent on the spectator's perception that his blood was real, his suffering was real, that he was a real and completely exposed naked body onstage. An escape from artifice, an escape from *costume* was central to his nudity, establishing a non-theatrical performance of suffering.

Through the mix of white make-up, repetitive sound and light, Franko's performances take on a mystical quality. The blood seeping from his arms draws on a set of religious referents, from St Sebastian to Christ, and there is a Catholic aspect to his attitude towards the body as the receptacle of an inner truth, and the idea of suffering having transubstantial effects on his presence. His work relies on the idea that nudity is a source of truth. Franko B's *thereness* in the art gallery, his bleeding and his nudity, allows the spectator imaginary access to the interior of the body. The performance foregrounds the usually invisible and visceral stuff of the body that we rarely see. His bleeding is established as an act of purging and salvation rather than desecration, and the ritual aspects of his performance suggest that nothing should get in the way of our access to his being, a being that is: 'an elegiac body of sorrows' (Jones, 2006, p. 1). This emphasis on nudity implies that costume would interrupt the body's truth in its temporal presence in performance. Speech, costume and theatrical representation are rejected as falsehoods.

However, we might wonder if the anointment of the body in white make-up means that Franko B's body can't help but enter a theatrical realm. As we saw in Chapter 2, once the body enters a designated space of art (a stage or a gallery), it becomes "a body", imbued with inverted commas within the heightened terrain of performance. It could be argued that Franko B's use of make-up works in a similar way to the ritual movement, costume and space of striptease. The make-up places his body at an aesthetic distance from the spectator along with the use of blood as make-up, the lighting, sound and dry ice. Even as Franko attempts to escape theatrically through nudity, what we see is the performance of honesty rather than a real body that has escaped representation. Honesty is the fantasy of his performance, just as it is the fantasy underlying the criticisms of Blair's fake tan. Franko's nudity imagines costume as a lie, but he positions the skin itself as a costume, a white shield (or "canvas" as he describes it), beneath which the truth – the blood – exists and is expressed. Franko B's performances imagine the body in similar ways to Stanislavski: an outer membrane that conceals inner truths, which are then expressed outwardly through the stimulus of the performance. Here, the skin is the membrane that covers up the truth of blood and tissue and pain.

What is crucial for this approach to nudity is that Franko B does not undress onstage: his body is not established through clothes. It is essential for the effect of honesty that he appear already naked in performance. Once his body is presented as already naked, there is no boundary crossed between his body and objects enacted by the removal or addition of dress. As a result, a decrease in status is not possible, so his nudity does not risk producing a comic effect. His body appears honest because it does not appear to be established through its relation to the status or hierarchy of clothes and dressed-ness. However, this argument does not take account of the white-coated and masked figures that stand at the sides of his performance, watching, intervening and eventually stringing him up. Their dressed state is reminiscent of the hooded figure in Beckett's *Not I*, who watches Mouth's failed workings with helpless compassion (see Beckett, 1986, p. 373). Here, however, the medical figures are sinister controlling ones, establishing the abjection and suffering of Franko B's bleeding body all the more through their clothed state. As a result, the effect of B's performance relies heavily on the distinction between his "honest", naked and abject body, and the clothed and masked figures that surround him. As with striptease, his body is rendered more naked by being surrounded by clothes. Once again, nudity is the product of clothing onstage.

Celebrity Striptease

In the past 15 years or so, the stages of the West End in London, and Broadway in New York, have been littered with the bodies of nude celebrities. Daniel Radcliffe's naked turn in *Equus* was only one of many undressing scenes involving a film star onstage. In 2000 Kathleen Turner undressed onstage in *The Graduate* in London's West End, while in 1998, Nicole Kidman took off all her clothes in *The Blue Room* at the Donmar Warehouse in London. Somewhat like Franko B's emphasis on honesty, celebrity nudity onstage promises to reveal a truthful presence: to peel away the layers of artifice that usually clothe the star. The performance's promise is that, when watching *The Graduate*, you will "really see" Kathleen Turner naked. The idea of the real body is at the centre of what is being sold. Liveness is continually cited by journalists to explain the overwhelming desire of audiences to view Turner, or Kidman, or Radcliffe onstage with their collective kits off, in an era where naked bodies abound in films, on the internet and in magazines. Theatre's immediacy is cited as the reason that audiences flock to view the movie star naked onstage, such as when Thomas Sutcliffe described the effects of nudity in *The Independent* as: 'a testimony to the unique intimacy of the theatre, a place where the exposure of the actor – bodily and emotional – can't be protected by retakes or retouching' (Sutcliffe, 2006, p. 28).

However, while the liveness of the event appears to be at the heart of the appeal of the naked celebrity, in fact quite the opposite effect takes place in the theatre. Nudity, it turns out, is just another trick to shore up the starriness of the celebrity. Nudity feeds the fantasy of the real, which is at the heart of the star system, but it doesn't actually reveal the real as promised. We saw in Chapter 1 how the "real" actor is actually an outcome of the performance, an illusion that runs alongside the illusion of the character. We might imagine the presence of the star actor as "uber-real", their celebrity making "realness" central to their presence. Michael Quinn points out in his essay, 'Celebrity and the Semiotics of Acting' (1990), that the celebrity actor exerts a Brechtian alienation effect upon the illusion onstage, drawing the spectator's attention to the presence of their "real" selves, and interrupting the illusion of the character they are playing: 'the personal qualities of the individual actor dominate the perception of the actor's references to the fictional events' (Quinn, 1990, p. 155). Quinn suggests, therefore, that the "real" is an effect produced by the performance, and the presence of the celebrity actor has a disruptive effect on the fiction by constructing an alternative and competing illusion of presence on the stage.

Of course celebrities also carry the illusion of their past roles with them onto the stage. The continual confusion over whether audiences saw Radcliffe or Harry Potter undressing in commentaries about *Equus*, demonstrate that it is not necessarily the "real" actor that the audience want to see naked. The titillation inbuilt in the scene was mixed up with the fact that Harry Potter is, somewhat disturbingly, a famous character from a children's book and film whose now grown-up readers and viewers attended the show. The seeming reality of the celebrity's presence in naked performance has very little to do with who the actor really is: rather the spectator's perception of celebrity actors is formed by the residue of their previous roles, which shapes the reception and enjoyment of their nakedness.

We can now see that the effects on presence that we identified of stage nudity at the beginning of this chapter can contribute to the fantasy of the presence of the "real" celebrity, a fantasy that is central to the star system. In this, the naked celebrity onstage has the appearance of offering the unmediated qualities of stage presence "for real". Here, however, the theatrical becomes the alibi for the real: it's what permits the fantasy of the real to appear. Even if stage nudity appears to offer the salvo of immediacy, the film star's body onstage is already layered with filmic or televisual reference points. Film and television situate the spectator in a completely different temporal and spatial relationship with actors to theatre, and so when film stars enter the stage, they are dislocated by their associations with these other art-forms. The event of the nude celebrity is sold on the promise of their presence in the real time and space of theatre, but they remain remote and unavailable.

In fact, might it be that these mediated and absent qualities are precisely the reasons for the naked celebrity's theatrical success? Perhaps actors known from film and television roles make it easier for the audience to take voyeuristic pleasure in their naked bodies? Spectators carry their way of looking at film into the theatre, while simultaneously relishing the promise of real life presence. The tease in this form of stripping is centred on the fluctuation between filmic and theatrical modes; now we see Daniel Radcliffe onstage, now we see Harry Potter on film. The film star does not threaten to "look back", to break the frame of the illusion, or to demonstrate awareness of being watched, and as a result, ogling their naked body is much safer than looking at an unknown stage actor who might possibly acknowledge being viewed. The fact that looking voyeuristically is made possible by the celebrity actor is evinced by the anecdote of a spectator's mobile phone ringing during a performance of *This is Our Youth*, starring the (fully clothed) Hollywood actors Matt Damon and Casey Affleck in 2002. The audience member answered her phone and said loudly: 'They're right in front of me. I could reach out and touch them' (IMDB, 2002, p. 1). Damon asked her to call the person back. In this moment, the spectator was clearly unaware that the actor could hear her or see her: she had translated Damon's presence into cinematic time and space. Despite her excitement that he was "right there" in front of her, her association of this actor with celluloid clearly meant that she did not feel that she was "right here" in front of him. The anecdote illustrates the tendency to dress the celebrity's body in a cinematic coating.

Given the celebrity's coating in the mediation of film, it's notable that none of these celebrity nudes simply arrived onstage undressed. Rather, each performed the act of undressing, and dressing in full view of the audience. The removal of costume provided the required erotic effect, but it also meant that these stars could look like their familiar iconic selves to begin with. Their stripping unpeeled away the layers of the familiar iconic star body, in order to heighten the revelation of the bare body beneath. The costumes were essential in lending the body its nudity *and* its celebrity status. Here, lighting was also important: the visibility in each performance was murky, rendering the naked body almost invisible. This dim lighting might not have been a protection of the performer's (and audience's) modesty, so much as a further dimension of the tease. The body is seen in a half-light, allowing the audience wonder: 'is it really them?', 'am I *really* seeing Nicole Kidman nude?' The lighting, the costume, and most importantly, the mediated qualities of the performer's body, enabled the audience to take up the role of the voyeur with ease, with the mediated qualities of the celebrity body facilitating their pleasure in looking, leading one critic to describe Kidman as "theatrical Viagra" (Spencer, 2002, p. 10). Here, the relationship between commodification and pleasure is explicit in the celebrity turn: nudity sells the celebrity, and the celebrity sells nudity.

Nudity in celebrity performance, therefore, is a means to shore up the fantasy of the "real" star: the idea that we might somehow access who the actor "really is" by seeing them at their livest and most vulnerable onstage. The effects of stage nudity on presence ensure that this star status is supported. As we have seen with Daniel Radcliffe, the nude scene is often established towards the end of the performance, making the undressing similar to the star's grand entrance. Celebrities get naked, but their undressing is equivalent to wearing the best clothes onstage, and their nudity ensures that it is the fantasy of their presence that is most prominent in the reception of their performance. Nudity offers up the promise of the real, the revelation of truth, but invokes instead only further layers of stardom.

Weary Nudity

On the cover of this book is a picture of two naked men. They hold silver stars that look like props from a school play. The stars are badly made, probably out of cardboard and tinfoil. The men look contemplative, reflective, perhaps a little bored. It's unclear if they are in character, if this is a scene from a narrative or plot (a nativity play gone badly wrong perhaps?), but the homemade qualities of the stars and the faint boredom of the actors' expressions suggests that it's unlikely: somehow their postures don't suggest actors "acting", but rather, performers performing. The image is funny rather than erotic: the fact that they have coyly positioned stars over their penises draws attention to their nudity without necessarily titillating or teasing (although, this might not be the case if the performers were women). Their nudity is bluntly presented, the lighting is bright and they don't seem particularly ritualised, but at the same time, the artificial juxtapositioning of homemade stars with penises makes this scene clearly theatrical.

This is a photograph from the production *Bloody Mess*, a show which was made by the British theatre company Forced Entertainment in 2004. The boredom on the performers' faces is not unusual: Forced Entertainment's work expresses a weariness with theatricality, but not a complete rejection of it. In their world, there is nothing else. The company, famed for their deconstructive approach to representation in performance offered snapshots of their trademark imagery: clowns, animal costumes and line-ups of actors directly addressing the audience; all in the context of a show that centred on 'a deep ambivalence towards the unintelligible and unknowable forces operating at a cosmic, as well as a micro, level' (Hoffman, 2006, p. 701). The logic of failure was central to the structures of the show: the failure to represent, the failure of the audience to understand and the failure of the performers to understand each other. This logic permeated the uses of nudity on the stage. The production featured a wide range of different kinds of nakedness: nudity in dance; the labour of dressing and undressing; imaginary nudity and already-undressed male nudity. However, nudity failed to move the audience; it didn't offer salvation, or truth or even erotic pleasure. Its uses often collapsed, or failed to make meaning in performance, and ultimately the performance demonstrated a sense of weariness with the supposedly transgressive power of the naked onstage. Audiences were expected to be resolutely unimpressed, or only mildly entertained, by the undressed performers in this show.

At the beginning of the performance Cathy Naden, wearing a pink evening dress, lay on the floor as a corpse, while Terry O'Connor performed repetitive gestures of grief at her death, wailing over the body, while dancing to *Born to Be Wild*, throwing water over herself and shaking her breasts out of her dress. Every so often, O'Connor would choose a different dress from the rack of costumes onstage and change into it, leaving her boots and knickers on in between changes. Her act of dressing and undressing was workmanlike – she did not tease the audience with her stripping, but rather performed the work of dressing, offering the audience a self-conscious glimpse of the mundane work of the dressing room. Dance, therefore was presented as artificial, whereas dressing and undressing were offered as "real" actions. Dressing was a mechanical, working act, and while O'Connor's bare breasts might have been viewed initially as erotic by the audience the ritualised repetition of the dance quickly de-eroticised her nudity by rendering the act of exposure mechanical.

By contrast, the moment in the production that this photograph has captured featured Jerry Killick and Davis Freeman dancing onstage naked, holding their silver stars. They went on to suggest that the audience should enjoy a beautiful silence during the show, proceeding to describe the possible qualities of this silence. Ranging from the pause before making a wish, to the quiet moment after a car crash, or the hush when an astronaut is lost in space, the performers took it in turns to describe their silence while smiling lovingly and intimately at one another. These were imagined silences of tragedy and loss that were offered up with great affection by the two performers. The outcome was very funny in the contrast between their nakedness, their smiles, their stars and their speech.

This comic effect was heightened by the coyly placed stars around their groins, which occasionally "accidentally" lifted to reveal their penises. It was the absent-mindedness of the performers' nudity that was at the heart of its comedy. As Henri Bergson argues: 'the comic is that side of a person which through its peculiar inelasticity conveys the impression of pure mechanism, of automatism, of movement without life' (Bergson, 2008, p. 39). In this case, the seeming object of the body, its occasional dreamy assertion into the conversation, contrasted with the subjectivity of what the performers said: the comedy relied on a divide between the body and speech. Crucially, as a result, for much of the time the men's bodies were not objects, were not ritually repetitive, like O'Connor's, but were rather naked bodies that spoke. The production appeared to retain some of the gender divisions of naked identity – men as active speakers, whose nudity is coy and comic, and women as mute aesthetic objects, whose nudity is potentially erotic. Speech acted like clothing: it made the body comically naked but also made the male performers subjects, in control of their bodies and the stage space.

However, for the female performers, speech worked as a defence against the audience's voyeuristic gaze, resisting the audience's desire or ability to objectify their bodies. The female performers broke out of their costumed roles and directly confronted the audience. Claire Marshall, who had stated her intention for the audience to be 'utterly consumed by physical desire for me' (Forced Entertainment, 2004), at the beginning of the show, subsequently dressed up in a gorilla suit. Occasionally she removed her gorilla head in order to invite the audience to 'think [...] about your naked body next to my naked body' (Forced Entertainment, 2004), producing an imaginary naked, highly sexualised body "beneath" the gorilla suit. The comic tension between the tawdry animal suit and the sexually clichéd nature of the speech undermined the spectator's ability to achieve an all-powerful voyeuristic gaze at the female bodies on the stage. Unlike the supposed absorption of the dancer in the act of striptease, which facilitates the voyeuristic gaze, here Marshall resisted that gaze by turning herself into an animal, and by looking back at the audience, taunting them with the sorts of fantasies that are often invoked by stripping.

Just as the gorilla invited the audience to sexualise her invisibly naked body (thus calling into question both the audience's imagination and their ability to "look"), Cathy Naden also disrupted the image of "diva" presented by her red evening dress, by pleading with the audience. She told them: 'don't look at me [...] please stop looking at me [...] I don't want you to look at me now' (Forced Entertainment, 2004). Naden's mythic femininity, established by her costume, was disrupted by her speech: she demonstrated the ability to look back actively at the spectator. This strategy confronted the potentially objectifying gaze of the spectator, while simultaneously failing. After all, by telling the audience to stop looking at her, they inevitably did the opposite – the instruction trained the spectator's gaze on Naden, and it was the tension between the command and the actuality that rendered the audience's awareness of how they watched uneasy and self-conscious.

Nudity itself was framed as an uneasy act. In the case of Killick and Freeman, their project failed. A beautiful silence, it turned out, was unachievable onstage. Even though the performers timed the silence with their watches, citing their shared time with the audience, the truth of presence that real time and nudity seem to offer (a truth central to the logic of Franko B's work and the promise of the naked celebrity) was shown to collapse. The real time of the silence was continually interrupted by the fictional goings-on of the other figures onstage. The gorilla made her way across the stage on wheels and kicked Freeman, while the roadie characters counted lights and tested the microphones. Real time onstage was continually interrupted by the illusion, just as the nakedness was continually interrupted by speech, and by new uses of costume. This production performed the failed promises of nudity: the failures of presence, of truth and of the real.

Fundamentally, this performance assumed that the audience would *not* be shocked or offended or titillated by nudity. The performance positioned the audience to recognise that nudity didn't really matter. At one point, when Killick's star rose up to show his penis, he was cautioned to adjust his "costume", because this was a "family show" (Forced Entertainment, 2004). The idea of the performance being a "family show" was a joke at shock's expense. The performance set up the gestures of transgression while dismissing the power of theatre to shock or transgress. This use of nudity was a form of post-modern weariness, contrasting with the concept of the nude body as a site of truth and salvation in performance art, or celebrity promise of the real. Perhaps too, unshocking nudity is a way to defend theatre by diminishing its possible effects: how could nudity possibly shock you, or even turn you on, it seemed to say; what does it really matter? Nudity then became a tired theatrical gimmick in *Bloody Mess*, presented as a series of empty gestures, a failed possibility for shock or transformation. The disappointments of nudity were at the heart of this production.

Nudity as Costume

When *Equus* opened in London in 2007, the *New York Times* ran an article called 'The Tale of Harry Potter and the Naked Role' where it interviewed some of the audience members after they had seen the show. One interviewee said: 'I thought, "Harry Potter! Where are your glasses?" ' while another said of her and her friends' experience: 'After we saw the play, we were like, "Oh, my God – we'll never be able to see Harry Potter in the same way again [. . .] we saw him naked!" ' (Lyall, 2007, p. 10). The audience had gone to see a show starring Daniel Radcliffe, but what they saw was Harry Potter taking his clothes off. These accounts say a lot about the disappointments of nudity at the theatre. Nudity might appear to be the exception to the indistinguishability between the actor and costume claimed by this book, promising to reveal the truth, or the real, promising to allow the spectator to see actors as they "really are". Nudity appears to offer honesty or revelation as its central logic. But the honesty, it turns out, is a fantasy and the revelation, when it comes is, finally, a disappointment. It reveals nothing, it is merely a phantasm of performance, another one of theatre's illusions that we strain to see past, hoping for a glimpse of what is beneath it or behind it. Once again, the real disappears into the illusion and it becomes clear that the absolute presence of nudity did not take place in spite of theatre's illusions, but because of them. Nudity in the end is not the shedding of costume, but another manifestation of costume onstage, another version of the actor's body at the theatre.

6

Dressing the Immaterial: Costume and the Problem of Ghosts

In Charles Dickens' 1861 novel *Great Expectations*, Pip goes to the theatre to see his friend Mr Wopsle play Hamlet. The production is amateur and unconvincing, not least when the ghost of Hamlet's father enters the stage:

> The late king of the country not only appeared to have been troubled with a cough at the time of his decease, but to have taken it with him to the tomb, and to have brought it back. The royal phantom also carried a ghostly manuscript round its truncheon, to which it had the appearance of occasionally referring, and that, too, with an air of anxiety and a tendency to lose the place of reference, which were suggestive of a state of mortality. It was this, I conceive, which led to the Shade's being advised by the gallery to "turn over!" – a recommendation which it took extremely ill. It was likewise to be noted of this majestic spirit that whereas it always appeared with an air of having been out a long time and walked an immense distance, it perceptibly came from a closely contiguous wall. This occasioned its terrors to be received derisively.
>
> (Dickens, 2008, p. 239)

The mockery of this failed performance is not limited to the ghost: the generous use of metal in the jewellery Gertrude wears leads to the audience describing her as a "kettledrum", while the playing of multiple roles by a single actor is received with a: 'general indignation taking the form of nuts' (Dickens, 2008, p. 240). However, it is the ghost who is the victim of Dickens' longest description, and it is the ghost's distinct failure to frighten the audience, or to appear dead, that is at the heart of Dickens' parody.

Ann Rosalind Jones and Peter Stallybrass suggest that, as belief in the supernatural began to recede after the Renaissance, ghosts onstage became more and more problematic (see Jones and Stallybrass, 2000, pp. 245–269).

By the nineteenth century, audiences did not greet the appearance of ghosts with pity and fear but responded with rather more cynicism, as Charles Dickens' description suggests. The problem for modern ghosts is that the stubborn materiality of the conditions of performance keeps on interrupting the illusion of the ghost's appearance onstage. This problem of materiality extends to the sound made by costume, as John Gielgud observed: 'it seems to be an impossibility to design silent armour for the Ghost, and consequently he is always dressed extremely vaguely and underlighted almost out of recognition' (cited in Jones and Stallybrass, 2000, p. 246). As Jones and Stallybrass point out, the great threat to the ghost on the twentieth-century stage is laughter: the clumsy intrusions of body, clanking armour, and the constraints of theatrical time and space, fundamentally disrupt the possibility of an audience believing that a ghost has appeared onstage.

Scholars have made much of the ghostly aspects of performance, citing in the (failed) repetitions, reappearances and disappearances of the theatre event, the essentially haunted nature of live performance. Not quite present, and not quite gone, theatre, like ghosts, repeatedly returns as the past in bodily form, combining remembrance and decay within a haunted spectacle. This interest in ghosting has permeated much theatre work since the late nineteenth century, from Ibsen and Strindberg's ghost sonatas, to the half-lives of Beckett's characters, to the intertextual recycling and hauntings of post-modern performance. Additionally scholars, such as Marvin Carlson, have investigated the role of memory in performance, acknowledging how the cumulative effects of previous shows will "haunt" the spectator's relation to the performance they watch at the theatre, ghosting the bodies of actors, the objects onstage and the reinterpretations of play texts and famous roles (Carlson, 2003, p. 2). However, while the deathliness of performance has been an ongoing concern for the artists and scholars of the twentieth century, there has been a much longer standing conundrum surrounding the relationship between costume and death. This has been the problem of what ghosts should wear in performance. While concepts of ghosting apply very well as metaphors for the theatre, the difficulty of dressing ghosts for the stage presents a problem for theatre's relationship with costume. The indistinguishability of actors and their costumes presents a conundrum for a stage moment, in which the costume *shouldn't* seem to have a body in it. The struggle with costuming ghosts might seem a rather narrow one, but this chapter is going to argue that it reveals a broader set of problems that are centred on costume's uncanniness. The peculiarity of clothes onstage comes to light when we think about dressing ghosts.

In a sense, the difficulty surrounding the costuming of ghosts belies the broader peculiarities of theatre costume that have been the study of this book. We have seen the multiple ways in which actors appear uncanny in costume. Costumed actors sometimes look like objects, or act as substitutes for absent identities, or seem more present, and yet all the more artificial, when naked. Most of the time, the peculiarities of costume don't take centre stage, they only operate at the corner of the spectator's eye. Nonetheless, at times in performance the aspect of costume's apparent indistinguishability from the body of the actor (its role in creating fleshliness and presence) may emerge in performance. At other times, this seamlessness is countered by costume appearing apparently autonomous as an object, which can be taken off, and this version of costume also has an uncanny quality. Costumes, then, have a peculiar half-life: they are not quite objects and not quite actors. Staging ghosts makes this half-life glaringly obvious. When costume is required to establish the presence of a ghost, its own uncanny state becomes evident. Costume is obviously material when clothing the immaterial ghost: its "thereness" interrupts the illusion of the "not-there". Staging ghosts poses a particular problem for theatre: how can clothes, with their suggestion of flesh and presence, costume a figure that is characterised by bodilessness and absence?

Of course, costumes are always taking on this task. After all, they flesh out theatre characters all the time, characters that are like ghosts themselves, in their theatrical half-lives, only emerging from the shadows when a play is in progress. However, stage ghosts make this process visible, making dress appear to be both a "thing" and a person. Ghosts throw the relationship between the illusion and the real, between the ghost, and the actor who plays him, into disarray. The nineteenth-century desire, expressed in Dickens' novel, to watch uninterrupted, to be absorbed into the spectacle, is fundamentally disrupted by a form of costume that is resistant to absorption, by an instance where some thing of the world (clothing) is used to costume something not of the world (a ghost). The problem of costume is at the heart of the trouble with staging ghosts.

We can think about this trouble in a number of ways. First the history of the ghost in *Hamlet* is worthy of consideration for the ways in which it traces out an ongoing attrition of the material impact of costume on the stage. Furthermore, a history of Hamlet's reaction to the ghost offers a particularly rich account of costume's connection with interiority and the self. It is also worth considering the broader interest in death and the ghostly in modernist and post-modernist performance. I'm going to look in particular at three productions that have dwelt on the un-dead qualities of costume and make-up: Ron Vawter's *Roy Cohn/Jack Smith*, The Wooster Group's *Brace Up!* and Forced Entertainment's production *Spectacular*. Finally, I'm going to examine the curtain call, to suggest that the actor bowing is a particularly uncanny and ghostly figure through the continuing presence of the character's costume on the stage.

Dressing Ghosts

Why would it be specifically the nineteenth century when staging ghosts become so difficult? Dickens assumes that it's the messy theatricality of the failed production of *Hamlet* that gets in the way of the audience's suspension of disbelief. However, the resistance to the ghost in Mr Wopsle's production may also be an outcome of the ambiguity of ghosts in nineteenth-century culture. There was a certain suspension of *belief* in ghosts at this time. The emerging secular principles of the culture began to erode the widespread belief in ghosts. However, this is not to say that ghosts no longer featured in the wider cultural consciousness: it is as if they were pushed out to the margins of the culture, haunting the borders between acceptable and unacceptable belief. We can see this ambiguity in Freud's careful mention of ghosts in his 1919 essay "The Uncanny": 'all supposedly educated people have ceased to believe officially that the dead can become visible as spirits and have made any such appearances dependent on improbable and remote conditions' (2003, p. 365). Freud's use of the word "official" suggests a complex relation of belief and power surrounding ghosts, perhaps best summed up by an apocryphal anecdote of the Irish Farmer in the 1950s who, when asked if she believed in fairies replied indignantly: 'I do not sir – but they're there anyway' (cited in Kiberd, 1996, p. 2).

As a result, ghosts were socially ambiguous figures on the stage: it was not quite clear if the actor playing a ghost was representing a real figure beyond the stage, or simply a fantasy of the performance. Perhaps it's the fact that ghosts are not quite fictional, that poses the central challenge for costuming them. If we were quite certain that there was no such thing as ghosts, then the stuff of costume would work very happily to clothe the unbelievable, since there wouldn't be any constraints on how the ghost might appear or what he might be made of. On the other hand, if we aren't sure we believe in ghosts, then things onstage (like armour and actors) become ambiguous too – costuming ghosts becomes a hesitant and unclear act. By the nineteenth century, ghosts were expected to appear to disappear onstage, as Jones and Stallybrass argue: 'at the historical point at which ghosts themselves become increasingly implausible [...] it seems to be necessary to assert their immateriality, their invisibility. The grosser the signs of materiality, the more the observers are likely to detect fraud and imposture'

(Jones and Stallybrass, 2000, p. 248). However, even while ghosts were expected to seem immaterial or invisible onstage, they were still expected to be frightening, suggesting that they continued to have a cultural force despite their officially implausible status.

Perhaps, though, this problem emerges most powerfully in the staging of *Hamlet*, which specifically requires that the ghost should wear armour. Other Shakespeare plays that contain the supernatural, like *Macbeth* or *A Midsummer Night's Dream*, don't prescribe the costume of other worldly characters so directly. So, what we might see in Gielgud's observation about the problem of armour's noisiness is less a symptom of the loss of audience belief in ghosts, and more a symptom of the loss of the audience's understanding of the signifier of *armour* as a ghostly and terrifying thing on the stage. Jones and Stallybrass, and R. A. Foakes have investigated the deeply resonant role that armour played in systems of inheritance and masculinity in the early modern period (see Jones and Stallybrass, 2000, pp. 245–269 and Foakes, 2005, pp. 34–48). Armour brought onto the Renaissance stage a whole host of connections and complexities, not least the faint suspicion in *Hamlet* that this might be a Catholic ghost appearing to a Protestant son, as Stephen Greenblat argues so eloquently (2001, p. 240). What we see (or hear) in the clanking armour, is a decaying sign, a sign that is haunted by the loss of its own history. Audience belief relies, not necessarily on a social belief in ghosts (since audiences will frequently agree to believe in much more absurd things than ghosts on the stage) but rather on a loss of belief in the apparatus that produces the ghost.

This loss is especially a loss of belief in the ability of clothing to resonate with social meanings and remembrance, in the ways that it did in the Renaissance. Perhaps the biggest problem with the ghost of Hamlet's father for contemporary audiences is that he renders clothing visibly instrumental in the expression of his past self. As we saw in Chapters 2 and 3, the move to a model of interiority during the nineteenth century meant that a new and paradoxical attitude to clothes emerged, in which dress was the receptacle for a self that was not found in clothing, but was nonetheless reflected by it. It's no accident that it is in a nineteenth-century novel that Hamlet's father is pilloried: it is in this moment that clothing is no longer considered adequate for the representation of the self. Armour no longer works as a ghostly object; it gets in the way of a broader cultural demand for the theatrical means to represent the self in immaterial and interior ways – a demand we saw manifest itself in the modernist approach to actors and objects. We can see in the hesitancy about costuming contemporary ghosts, a larger hesitancy about the conventions of representing the (lost) self through clothes (see Jones and Stallybrass, 2000, pp. 245–269).

Dickens' critique also appears to rely on the classical tradition of theatrical bodilessness, where, as Henri Bergson suggests, 'no sooner does anxiety about the body manifest itself than the intrusion of a comic element is to be feared. On this account, the hero in a tragedy does not eat or drink or warm himself. He does not even sit down any more than can be helped' (Bergson, 2008, p. 15). Indeed, Dickens' parody is at the expense of the actor's bodily interruptions of the ghost's illusion. However, his guiding principles for this critique are not based on a set of classical precepts, but are instead predictive of the realism to come on the stage, and already at work in the Victorian novel. The desire for the ghost to operate in a coherent relationship to social (rather than theatrical) time and space looks forward to realism, rather than back to Aristotle. Dickens' parody requires a new set of theatrical conventions, in which ghosts can be staged as internal, linguistic and metaphorical qualities, rather than as manifestly material figures. Dickens requires a theatrical logic in which new kinds of ghosts can occupy invisibly the terrain of real chairs and tea-cups, a terrain that was to emerge with a vengeance in Ibsen's play *Ghosts*.

By the end of the twentieth century, and the beginning of the twenty-first century, as Gielgud intimates, the costuming of old kinds of ghosts often entails skipping the armour entirely and going straight for the nightgown. Jones and Stallybrass suggest that the long history of ghostly attrition reached its zenith in a Royal Court production in London in 1980, where Jonathan Pryce's Hamlet was possessed by the ghost of his father, who emerged like a satanic force through the actor's contorted body and voice. Pryce became the costume for the ghost: the fabric of his body materialising the presence of Hamlet's father. The ghost was internalised, an embodiment of the twentieth-century tendency to psychologise Hamlet's relationship with his parents, as a critic summarised of the production: 'one Freud would have enjoyed' (Billington, 1994, p. 17). Pryce's performance offered a solution for a world where ghosts no longer exist officially: ghosts are now presented onstage as coherently immaterial, uninfected by the constraints of time and space in performance.

Reactions to Ghosts

As the ghost's presence onstage diminished after the Renaissance, so Hamlet's *reaction* to the ghost became more and more central to the scene. It is as if the audience's fear needed to be relocated, because the ghost could no longer present a frightening enough figure in his own right. The actor's performed response then, became a substitute ghost: producing the correct feelings of terror in the audience, without relying on belief in theatrical spectres. This response was also centred on a relationship to costume. Shock at the entrance of the ghost was first made famous by David Garrick in 1742, when his violent start at the appearance of the ghost was heralded as a terrifying example of his actorly prowess. Georg Christoph Lichtenburg described the action:

> Garrick turns sharply and at the same moment staggers back two or three paces, with his knees giving away under him; his hat falls to the ground and both his arms, especially the left, are stretched out nearly to their full length, with the hands as high as his head, the right arm more bent and the hand lower and the fingers apart; his mouth is open; thus he stands rooted to the spot.
>
> (cited in Roach, 1993, pp. 86–87)

Lichtenberg, however, misses out a crucial ingredient in the scene. At the entrance of the ghost, the hairs on Garrick's wig stood on end (see Figure 6). Audiences reported the effect to be terrifying (Roach, 1993, p. 58). Garrick had invented a fright-wig for the scene, one that could express the full power of Hamlet's horror at the entry of the ghost, by rising up to greet it. As Joseph Roach puts it: 'Hamlet, Prince of Denmark, flipped his wig' (Roach, 1993, p. 58). While Marcellus's line from Hamlet: 'what, has this thing appeared again tonight?' refers to the ghost, and has been interpreted by Freddie Rokem as a commentary on theatre itself (cited in Carlson, 2001, p. 7), in this instance it might also be a question asked by Garrick's audiences, for what a very odd thing the wig was. Working by a hydraulic mechanism, the "thingliness" of the wig – its apparent animation – and its autonomy in expressing and invoking fear – had its own ghostly properties: it was not alive and yet it was not dead. Its uncanniness, an effect that Freud defines as combining the frightening and the familiar (Freud, 2003, p. 364) enacted fear mechanically, enhancing and expressing Garrick's emotional power.

In its eighteenth-century context, the wig stands as a testimony to the power of clothing in the culture, and on the stage. As we saw in Chapter 2, innovations in costume in the eighteenth century were attributed to the actor's art rather than to the tailor's work, or the actor–manager's aesthetic vision. Costume and acting were inextricably linked, and viewed as the expression of the actor's genius. As Anne Hollander argues, changes to costume: 'were memorable [...] not as [aesthetic] innovations but as attributes of individually excellent performances' (Hollander, 1993, p. 281). Actors and audiences treated the body as a frame for innovation and fashion: both wore public clothing to the theatre, with theatre costumes often working as a proving ground for new fashions on the street (see Sennett, 1976, p. 40). Furthermore, as Joseph Roach argues, the eighteenth-century

Figure 6   Garrick. tragédien Anglais ne en 1716, mort en 1779. (Rôle d'Hamlet.) Galerie Universelle. publiee par Blaisot. (Ducarme, Lithograph, date unknown, by permission of the Shakespeare Folger Library).

scientific models of the body viewed it as a physiological machine, as 'a statue mechanically endowed with motion' (Roach, 1993, p. 68). Garrick's wig operated as an extension of this scientific metaphor, working as an outer mechanical instrument of emotion that mimicked, and expressed, the internal workings of the body. Additionally, Garrick's *Hamlet* was interspersed by other theatrical events that were also focused on costume, with: 'a grand comic dance by Signor Checo Torinese and Signora Chiaretta Aquilanti, Signor Boromeo, Madem. Bonneval and others' after Act II (*Hamlet* playbill, 1742, p. 1). Garrick's performance of Hamlet's shock took place within a spectrum of displays of virtuosity that also employed highly elaborate and artificial costumes. Costumes in the eighteenth century were central to actors' power, and their art, and shock at the ghost was therefore naturally embodied by a wig.

However, by the time we come to Mr Wopsle's fictional turn as Hamlet in Dickens' novel, the costume is no longer considered capable of producing terrifying effects for Hamlet's shock at the ghost. When Pip and his friend make a trip backstage to visit Mr Wopsle once the play has ended, Wopsle's servant and dresser critiques his performance based on how badly he showed off his costume: ' "When he come to the grave, [. . .] he showed his cloak beautiful. But, judging from the wing, it looked to me that when he see the ghost in the queen's apartment, he might have made more of his stockings" ' (Dickens, 2008, p. 241). Costumes are torn away from the actor's art. The idea that showing one's stockings might be a sign of good acting is laughable, and again the novel suggests that costume interrupts, rather than sustains, the emotional effects of performance.

We can see this erosion of the role of costume in the representation of Hamlet's shock, in Sarah Bernhardt's enactment of Hamlet in 1899. Bernhardt's performance was heralded as an innovation in its own right: her cross-dressed turn took place within a nineteenth-century interest in star performance. However, by this time, the tradition of Hamlet's reaction to the appearance of the ghost was so well established, that Bernhardt was forced to defend her Hamlet's *lack* of shock, in a letter to the *Daily Telegraph*: 'I am reproached with not being suitably astonished, not sufficiently dumb-founded, when I see the ghost. But Hamlet comes expressly to see it; he awaits it' (Bernhardt, 1889). Notably, Bernhardt's performance choices did not rely on innovative uses of costume, or scientific attitudes to shock, as in Garrick's case. Now, the logic of character psychology and textual evidence were at the nub of the discussion. Bernhardt's costume did not function to create emotion in the audience, or to bolster her virtuosity. Instead, it con-tributed to her attractiveness and star status on the stage, as the critic from the *Globe* put it:

> In appearance, Mdme Bernhardt is graceful. No question arises concerning Ham-let being fat or scant of breath. With her fair hair clustering around her head, a short tunic apparently of black silk trimmed with sable, black hose, and a long and flowing silk cloak, she is the ideal of a young prince.
>
> (*Globe*, 1889)

Now costume worked as an adjunct to the star's attractiveness, no longer central to the actor's demonstration of virtuosity. Instead, Bernhardt's innovations and actorly prowess were located in her use of textual logic and in her mental preparations for the performance. Newspapers reported that Bernhardt prepared by rehearsing on the battlements of a deserted castle at night: 'she left Paris and betook herself to her chateau in Nor-mandy, where she paced the battlements in the moonlight and mentally conjured up before her the wraith of that dead king of Denmark whose behests she strives to comprehend' (*Daily Mail*, 1889). Costume no longer had the ability to communicate power or virtuosity – it simply supple-mented the interior world of the actor produced through rehearsal and preparation.

By the time of Pryce's performance in 1980, Hamlet's reaction to the ghost had seamlessly morphed into a manifestation of the ghost itself. The drive towards a dematerialised approach to clothing seemed to have reached its height. Pryce's performance simultaneously worked as a metaphor for the practice of acting itself, or at least a post-Stanislavskian notion of acting, in which an actor is possessed and inhabited by a character, and rendered helpless against its force. We saw Stanislavski's approach to the actor in Chapter 3, where costume works as a mask that infects the unconscious. The meanings of the exterior of the body invade the interior, whose truths rise to the surface, in the form of a fever or a dream. In Pryce's performance, the character of the ghost functioned like Stanislavski's costume: Hamlet was rendered actorly by the possession and expression of his father's spirit.

Furthermore, Pryce himself was attributed with the qualities he performed. A critic described him as: 'a lean saturnine figure with a whippet-like body and a piercing eye' (Billington, 1994, p. 7). Unlike Garrick's Hamlet, where the innovation of costuming lent him status as a "great actor" in performance, Pryce's innovation was imagined to remake the actor as both powerful and ghostly. The modern assumption that characters haunt the psyche of actors resulted in a re-moulding of Pryce's intertextual figure. Here, the actor's body is formed by a character's psyche that is not of his body, but is situated within it, just as the ghost is not of Hamlet's body but emerges from it. The figure of Pryce was imagined to have been haunted by his role so much that it re-modelled the contours of his face and body.

Modern and Post-Modern Ghosts

The traditions of costuming Hamlet and the ghost trace out the growing tendency to repress the materiality of costume in favour of an interiorised model of identity. Pryce's performance can be seen as the culmination in a long history of "reactions to ghosts", in which costume begins to disappear as the actor's central expression of fear. The traditions of costuming the ghost and Hamlet are revealing of the relationship between theatre's attitude to objects and materiality, and the history of signs. This chapter has suggested so far that the attrition of the importance of costume forms a relatively unbroken line from the eighteenth century to the end of the twentieth century. However, the approach to costumes in modernist and post-modernist theatre constitutes a break with this historical trajectory.

As we saw in Chapter 3, costume and make-up have often been used to invoke deathliness in twentieth- and twenty-first-century performance, with a particular focus on the power of the mask to function as a medium for the dead. Mary Wigman saw in masks: 'something so remote and beyond life that I could visualise for it only motionless silence' (cited in Melzer, 1994, p. 98), while Antoine Artaud praised Balinese costume for how: 'the stiff stilted artist seems merely his own effigy' (Artaud, 1970, p. 41). As we have seen in chapter 3, Modernist artists frequently posited the use of the mask as a cure for social ills: as a means to alleviate the sicknesses of the century. Costumes were imagined as a source of insight into the ghostly aspects of performance, and the broader spiritual dimensions of the world: not only for the actor but, most importantly, for the audience. Here, the thing became the a priori of the actor. Halting the trajectory of Garrick's wig to Bernhardt's decorative costume to Pryce's internalisations, the modernist artist reversed the historical tendency to repress the materiality of costume, in favour of the uncanny object of the mask.

Taking their cue from the Naturalist investment in the realm of objects as a source of truth, as we saw in Chapter 3, Modernist artists made a further leap, by imbuing objects with metaphysical properties, which are served by, rather than serving, the actor's work. Perhaps we can see in the repression of the actor's presence in the twentieth century, something strangely akin to the problem of costuming ghosts in the nineteenth century? Just as the ambiguity of belief in ghosts demands an immateriality in performance, perhaps too, the early twentieth-century loss of faith in the unified human subject – in the possibility of presence – begins to manifest itself in the preference for objects over actors? The actor's body is now considered too theatrically messy for *any* role, not just for ghosts, and costumes and objects take over the function of invoking terror and insight into mortality. Furthermore, costumes begin to situate the actor within a specific field of labour – costumes produce and assume certain kinds of theatrical work that is determined and delimited by its structures and design. In this case, costumes wear the actor rather than the other way round, and take on a life of their own.

There is a melancholic yearning built into these modernist costume, as Avery Gordon suggests that: 'haunting always harbours [...] the exile of our longing, the utopian' (1997, p. 207). However, after World War II, attitudes to objects changed again. The half-lives of Beckett's characters (often described as if they are in purgatory – see Suvin, 1967, pp. 23–36) are emphasised by the ordinariness of their clothing. The bowler hats, straw hats, handbags, grey dresses and morning suits, do not ground the characters in a realist universe, or offer the audience transcendence, but rather render them other-worldly. The costumes in conjunction with mounds, and trees, and shafts of light, are rendered relic-like: fragments from another time or a previous life. Winnie's straw hat and décolletage become an act of remembrance and absurdity when she is trapped in a mound (see Beckett, 1986, p. 135). The characters' insistence on the meanings of these things, and the things' continual failure (the falling trousers, the burning parasols) are visibly fragile and hopeless attempts to render a meaningless and cruel world somehow logical. These characters are caught between life and death, like ghosts, and their costumes are remainders and reminders of a forgotten past and an impossible future. Just as the modernists in the earlier part of the century had rendered the human body an uncertain and unstable thing, the later modernists equally dismissed the possibility that costumes and objects might offer solace in an absurd universe (see Esslin, 1980).

A more recent example of the relationship between ghostliness and costuming can be seen in Ron Vawter's performance piece, *Roy Cohn/Jack Smith* in 1992. In this show, make-up returned the dead to the stage. Vawter, a founder member of The Wooster Group, impersonated two prominent public figures who died of AIDS in the 1980s. In the guise of Roy Cohn, the notoriously homophobic republican lawyer (who was a closet homosexual), he first delivered an imaginary hate-filled speech to the American Society for the Protection of the Family. In the second half of the show he reconstructed a performance art piece by Jack Smith, a downtown New York performance artist, who used highly elaborate costumes and make-up in his performances and films. Vawter was dying of AIDS when he performed these roles, a fact that he acknowledged in his introduction at the beginning of the performance. His approach to performance was centred on costuming.

When Vawter prepared for his role as Roy Cohn, he was fitted for a tuxedo by Cohn's tailor (see Schechner, 1998, p. 450). He not only wore a suit very similar to the figure he impersonated, Vawter also went through the same process of being measured and formed by the tailor's handiwork. This form of preparation echoes Kostya's in Stanislavski, where a material engagement with clothing is imagined to produce a transformative effect on the actor's psyche. However, unlike Kostya, where the aim is to convince the audience of his total transformation, Vawter played on the ambiguities of acting itself, making it unclear where he ended and Cohn began. This ambiguity could be seen in his (scripted) coughs when delivering Cohn's speech, which confused whose illness he was performing: Cohn's or his own.

Vawter recounted of his preparations to play Jack Smith that he had been given some of Smith's cremated ashes, and 'because Jack's sense of how to paint himself for a performance was so extreme, [...] I thought, well I'm going to use the ash, I'm going to return him to his own make-up. [...] So, I use the ash for every performance. I mix it with the glitter. I put it on my eyes and it charges me. It empowers me in a way that – I mean, when I'm sitting there and I know that Jack is on my face literally [...]

something spooky comes through' (Schechner, 1998, p. 451). Vawter wore the remains of Smith's body, in order to perform him: his make-up brought the dead back to the stage. Vawter's model of theatre as séance, and the mask as effigy, echoes the earlier modernist belief in the mask's ability to access the dead. In a post-AIDS universe, Vawter extended the modernist project by constructing and wearing a literal death mask: a mask made of the dead. Vawter also reiterated Stanislavski in his emphasis on make-up's ability to infect the actor's subconscious, with the ashes allowing 'something spooky come [...] through' (Schechner, 1998, p. 451). Vawter used an intentionally ghosted form of make-up, and in doing so, posited a peculiarly Catholic relationship with things. The make-up worked like a relic, it was alive with the presence of the dead. The Catholic qualities of this approach to things is no great surprise, given Vawter's background as an army chaplain, but this sensibility might also extend to a larger theatrical concern with the aliveness of dead objects, and the richly meaningful history of clothes. Somehow, inanimate remains can become transformative onstage, imbuing the body of the performer (and according to the Modernists, the spectator) with meanings, history and remembrance.

However, unlike the Modernist vision of the object as a social curative, Vawter used this make-up only to heal himself. The make-up's deathliness was a private, internal and meditative experience: the audience was not made aware of Jack Smith's presence as relic. Instead, Vawter's intention was for the performance to politicise and contextualise the AIDS crisis: 'I want to take two people with AIDS, go beyond that and continue with discussion about the forces of repression in this country' (Schechner, 1998, p. 453). Vawter approached the performance with a Brechtian impulse, intending that the impersonations should have an epic effect, situating AIDS within a wider political landscape. The ashes then, and their transformative effect on Vawter's psyche, were not politically or aesthetically instrumentalist, at least not based on the artist's stated intentions. Instead, the make-up retained its conventional post-Stanislavskian function in transforming the actor's appearance for the audience, and producing a private internal state for the performer. The ashes enabled a dying actor to commune with a dead one. Vawter's experience was enclosed, rather than collectively transformative. While the play offered an epic account of the social illnesses surrounding AIDS, the costume and make-up offered a different and transformative effect for the actor: an effect that was transcendental and ghostly: 'I get caught in a rhythm that is totally not mine, and that rhythm opens me up to a second will' (Schechner, 1998, p. 452).

The qualities of ghostliness in Vawter's relationship with costuming could also be found in the Wooster Group's production of *Brace Up!* in 2003. The avant-garde interest in costumes and death has been continued and extended by the Wooster Group. As we saw in Chapter 4, the company's uses of blackface and technology have produced various forms of masks that are overlaid on the actor's body, problematising the idea of an "original" face beneath the make-up or beyond the TV screen. In this production, the mask of technology summoned the dead to the stage. *Brace Up!* was loosely based on Chekhov's *Three Sisters*, and was first performed by the company in 1992. The 2003 production was a revival and re-imagining of the original show. In the intervening period, many of the performers from the 1992 production had died. Amongst these was Paul Schmidt, a professor of Russian literature and the translator of the Chekhov play, who also played Dr Chebutiken in the show. Schmidt died of an AIDS-related illness in 1999. Schmidt's death was foregrounded at the beginning of the show, when the actress Kate Valk introduced each actor and named the character they played. Introducing Schmidt, Valk informed the audience that he had died some years before, but that the company were lucky to have him on film. Turning to a video monitor, Valk said: "hi Paul", whereupon Schmidt's televised face turned to her and said: "hi Kate" (The Wooster Group, 2003).

Once again, a death mask enters the stage. In *Roy Cohn, Jack Smith*, Smith appeared through his own ashes, in a form of costumed ventriloquy, and in *Brace Up!* a dead man was seen speaking with his own voice. Of course, the audience couldn't know in any ontological sense that Schmidt really was dead – all they had to go on was the word of a theatre company famous for blurring the lines between truth and illusion. But, what they did experience was a death-effect: the act of telling the audience that Schmidt was dead was enough to invoke an uncanny kind of mask on the screen. Schmidt was described as dead, but was still performing: was simultaneously about to die, and already dead. This temporal confusion is an effect that Roland Barthes saw in photography, reading in a photo of a condemned man in 1897: 'he is going to die. I read at the same time: this will be and this has been; I observe with horror an anterior future of which death is the stake' (Barthes, 2000, p. 96). When the dead Schmidt spoke, his face was evacuated of being, and yet simultaneously overflowed with being, turning into a kind of ghostly mask, inhabiting a hinterland of past and future.

Schmidt was just one of many resurrected performers who haunted the Wooster Group's stage: footage of the late Josephine Buscemi as Anfisa the maid flickered across television screens, while other actors spoke live over video images of themselves from ten years earlier. Standing amongst the litter of images and voices of the dead, was Beatrice Roth, still alive at 84 years of age, playing Irina, the youngest sister of Chekhov's play. Roth was the only actor who was un-miked onstage, and her live voice struggled to compete with the mediated ones in performance. Roth, a denizen of the avant-garde theatre scene in New York, embodied a history of performances and artists now long gone and her performance moved from the comic (with audience laughter at her description as the "youngest sister") to the tragic when Irina mourned the passage of time and lost hopes in the third act. Roth became an embodiment of theatrical memory, her age and fragility manifesting the simultaneous presence and loss of the theatrical past. While Roth was surrounded by the technological masks of the dead, the one entirely invisible dead figure was Ron Vawter, who had performed the role of Vershinen in the original production and who died soon after the show. Vawter's presence haunted the production more keenly than any other through his complete absence in the performance, an absence felt by the company, and by the audience members who had seen the performance in its original incarnation.

However, it was Schmidt's death that was most powerfully presented to the audience, through Valk's framing of the video footage. Perhaps, though, there wasn't anything particularly unusual about the prospect of seeing a dead man speak on film. Indeed, maybe the Wooster Group simply made explicit the deathliness of all video footage?. A video recording suspends people in the past, who then emanate the suggestion of presence. Barthes suggests that this is the effect of the photograph, but the fact that the dead can *speak* on video, that they can *move*, makes the deathliness of the recorded media all the more uncanny. The conjunction of the live actor in conversation with the mask of a dead one, made the deathliness of mediation visible and central to the melancholic ruminations of the show. Schmidt's performance became a testament to the theatrical life that's gone and won't ever come back, the act of theatre's forgetting and the unceasing return of the dead to the stage.

Failed Ghosts

Forced Entertainment's 2008 production, *Spectacular* at the Riverside Studios in London, also put death and ghosts centre-stage. A man, "Robin", in a skeleton costume describes a performance that the audience cannot see, and a woman, "Claire", in seemingly everyday clothes announces that she will perform an agonising death scene, and proceeds to do so. In both cases, the deaths fail to convince. Indeed, this is the show's logic: it is almost as if the company are staging Dickens' parody of *Hamlet*. Standing on a bare stage, Robin tells the audience about the production that "normally" takes place (just not tonight): he describes the dancing girls, special effects, comic turns and musicians' stage personas, of the absent performance. The audience laugh. They laugh at the peculiar thing that theatre does: its tricks, its sincerities and its contractions of time and space. Robin's description of his "usual" first entrance down a set of stairs is particularly funny, in his assumption that his appearance frightens the audience (when he is so evidently not frightening) and in his extraordinarily lengthy entrance whose impact, as he describes it, is built up by music and lights. In the absence of a set, musicians or lighting effects, it is laughable that any of these moments could have the emotional drama that Robin describes. And so, just as Dickens laughs at the idea that ghosts could be frightening onstage, the audience laugh at the idea that theatre's illusions could be as moving as Robin suggests.

The laughter is particularly directed at Robin's skeleton costume, which is badly made and clearly fake. The outline of the skeleton is drawn onto one side of an ill-fitting and mismatching black tracksuit, which is slightly too small. The actor draws attention to this fact, gesturing to his beer belly as a particularly inappropriate piece of casting. After all, skeletons shouldn't be fat. In doing so, the actor also gestures to the oddity of actors playing skeletons at all. Any skeleton costume is going to be filled out, made fleshly and material by an actor, in ways that skeletons should not be. The idea that a representative of death could have a body, when ghosts and death *should* be immaterial (an assumption that, as we have seen, is historically specific), is at the centre of the joke of the costume, establishing its ludicrousness at the expense of theatre's ability to convince or frighten an audience.

Meanwhile, Claire's agonised death scene is another clearly artificial act. The fact that she announces that she will perform her "death" now, before lurching and gasping across the stage, suggests that the qualities of this death are at the heart of the failures and peculiarities of theatrical illusion. As the director, Tim Etchells, points out in a programme note: 'the strange game of playing dead [...] can't ever be convincingly represented. When we're at the theatre after all, once all the drama and exertions of the death scene are done, the actor is always still breathing as she lies there on the floor. Always still breathing, eyes closed and waiting patiently for the curtain call. No-one's fooled' (Etchells, 2008, p. 3). The death scene is a way of pointing out theatre's inadequacies, and its strangeness. This production sets up some classic scenes from the theatre: the death scene, the skeleton, the dancing girls and the dramatic entrance by staircase. These scenes are extracted from the logic of narrative or mise-en-scène that supports their meanings, and plonked onstage in isolation, (and sometimes only in language), for us to consider their inherent oddness. The production shows how peculiar these aspects of theatrical representation really are, suggesting that the uncanny and comical aspects of these scenes were always there to begin with.

However, in the midst all this tongue-in-cheek performance of theatre's inadequacies, something peculiar happens. The skeleton starts to look scary. Claire's agonising screams become disturbing. The peculiar aspects of theatre's attempts to move us begin to convince. How could this be? It is as if now only the vestiges of theatricality have the power to move us. Only when we relinquish the possibility of theatre having an emotional effect, can it do so. Now, the skeleton needs to fail before he frightens us: he must catch us unawares, rather than sincerely trying to be spooky. It is only once the fakeness of his costume has been acknowledged that he can become uncanny. His dark unreadable eye-sockets and the peculiar disembodied voice emanating from inside his mask shouldn't be frightening. But, every so often, a particular turn of his head, or a pause in his movement, makes his costume seem eerie and deathlike, as Etchells puts it: 'as if the patent absurdity of these things [...] always contains nonetheless a flicker, shimmer, crack or opening to some other possibility' (Etchells, 2008, p. 3). Ghostliness shimmers at the edges of the costume, occasionally emerging and then retreating once more into the peculiar mundanity of the act of pretending to be frightening.

The ghostly effects of the skeleton costume, and the disturbing repeated cries of Claire's anguish onstage, are rendered more uncanny again by the fact that they are both residues from previous Forced Entertainment shows. The skeleton tracksuit has been used many times by the company in its 24-year history, just as death scenes frequently feature in their work. The costume is ghosted by other performances and performers, while the death scene is familiar from other shows. These figures are already haunted with memories: ghosts of performances past. Of course, this effect is nothing special: after all, lots of companies reuse costumes and restage key scenes of haunting and death. Forced Entertainment however, makes it very clear that this is what they are doing: they make the ghostly qualities of costumes evident, just as Schmidt's appearance makes the deathly qualities of video evident. They do so, in order to point out, what a very peculiar and what a very powerful thing theatre is.

The Ghost in the Curtain Call

At the end of *Spectacular* the actors come onto the stage to take a bow. However, like the rest of the show, the bows seem ghostly. Towards the end of the show, Robin describes the curtain calls that "normally" take place in his absent performance, mimicking some of the musicians as they reluctantly come to the stage to bow, and describing the audience's applause. Now, *Spectacular* really has ended and the actors called Robin and Claire, who have just played characters called "Robin" and "Claire", take their bows. The borders of the performance are uneasily blurred; the bows refuse to remain distinct from the fiction and are stubbornly resistant to appearing real. The bows are permeated by the memory of what has just taken place. Bowing appears a remarkably ghostly activity.

In this, Forced Entertainment denies us the promise that bows seem to hold. Somehow, when actors bow, we imagine that they will reveal who they really are. They will no longer be the characters they have played: they will show us themselves, and in doing so, they will inculcate us into the mysteries of acting. Bows promise to help us find the seams between the actor and the illusion, and to tell us how they did it, to reveal what the trick was. But, just as the portraits of actors in their dressing rooms refuse us this satisfaction, so too, the actor's bow keeps its secrets to itself. The curtain call cannot divulge its secrets: all it does is establish new ones. The audience don't see the real actor, what they see is a performance by actors of their own presence. As Bert States describes it: 'the actor is, in a sense pretending that he is himself' (States, 1985, p. 203). The actor's bow is not a revelation of his/her "real" self but a further performance of "realness", which works within the frame of the illusion of the play, but is not part of it.

However, what is peculiar about bowing is how traces of the character stay within the actor's body, as States describes it:

> The character remains in the actor, like a ghost. It is not at all a clean metamorphosis. [. . .] We do not think of an actor's portrayal of a role as being sealed off in the past tense, but as floating in a past absolute, as it were, like the role itself, outside time. Not only is it preserved in the communal memory, as part of the history of the play, leaving its imprint (for a time) on the text, but due to the repetitive element in all style, remnants keep popping up in the later work of the actor.
>
> (States, 1985, p. 200)

What States describes as an "unclean metamorphosis" is at the heart of the ghostly qualities of the curtain call. The promise of the real actor is reneged on, and instead the audience is confronted by a composite and ambivalent figure who is neither one thing nor another: neither character nor real actor, neither costumed nor out of costume. Furthermore, States points out in this brilliant description of curtain calls (since first reading this passage, I now savour bows almost more than anything else when I go to the theatre) that characters don't just remain in actors during the bow: actors also remain in costume. Central to the ghostly aspects of the curtain call is the fact that actors don't take their stage body off when they take their bows. Actors are ghostly when they bow because they continue to embody their fading characters, who appear to have disappeared, but whose clothes remain onstage. They appear as indeterminate and unfinished "real" performers who are in costume but no longer in role. The actor bows in costume and that costume is reminiscent of Hamlet's father's armour: uncanny, unfilled and peculiar on the stage.

To make matters worse, theatre is also often in the habit of denying us even the closure of the disappearing character. As we saw in *Spectacular*, the actors are caught in a residue of the fiction: they are not distinct from it. This is particularly the case for the character and actor of Robin: all along the audience is told: "here is an actor in a skeleton suit." When the actor Robin comes onstage to bow, he has removed his mask. However, rather than seeing the "real" actor beneath the mask, we continue to see the fictional character of the actor-behind-the-mask. The real Robin is doubly denied to us, the character simply emerges in a new form. This effect is also true of Shakespeare's *Twelfth Night*. In the story of *Twelfth Night*, Viola cross-dresses as Cesario and gets into the usual trouble that romantic comedies demand. At the end of the play, the rightful order of sex and rank are restored: Cesario is discovered to be Viola, and gender and sex are put back in their rightful place. The act of crossing appears to have ended. However, on the stage during the curtain call on the Elizabethan stage, this was not so: the boy playing Viola took his bow in the costume of a girl playing a boy. The audience is denied seeing Viola in her "rightful" clothes, they continue to see her in costume, and so they are confronted with a composite of actor, role, character and costume that presents the uncanny and ghostly figure in the curtain call.

Ghostly Costumes

At the end of Mr Wopsle's failed attempts at Hamlet, Pip tries to applaud the production, but he laughs instead:

> We had made some pale efforts in the beginning to applaud Mr. Wopsle; but they were too hopeless to be persisted in. Therefore we had sat, feeling keenly for him, but laughing, nevertheless, from ear to ear.
>
> (Dickens, 2008, p. 241)

Ghosts, according to Dickens, don't work in the theatre. They no longer frighten us; they make us laugh instead. Indeed, the uncanny and comic dimensions of costume, that are always already in operation on the stage, become most apparent when they are clothing a ghost: the peculiarities of what actors do, or what they claim to do, become most evident when a ghost appears onstage. It turns out that Dickens was wrong, however. As a potted history of the avant-garde in the twentieth and twenty-first century shows us, just because being dressed in a sheet with cut-out eyes, or in armour no longer convinces, doesn't mean that ghosts have stopped appearing onstage or no longer frighten us. Ghosts might not succeed in convincing us because of the messy materiality of their costumes, but what Dickens fails to recognise is that we see ghosts all the time at the theatre: emerging through inheritance, reminding us of the dead, appearing in the curtain call. Actors bowing in leftover costumes stand as ghostly reminders of their theatrical bodies that once seemed so convincing. The applause that actors receive is applause for the mysteries of their art, for the unknowable strangeness of what they do and for the uncanny ability of costume to take on a life of its own. Actors always perform in costumes haunted by memory and forgetting, and the relic-like qualities of masks, make-up and badly fitting tracksuits continue to ensure that the dead will always come back to life on the stage.

Epilogue: After Effects –
Costume and the Memory
of Performance

On March 19, 1665, Samuel Pepys records in his famous diary a visit to the King's playhouse, which is undergoing renovations, and is lying empty. Pepys makes his way backstage to satisfy his curiosity about the secret world of the theatre, visiting the dressing rooms in a journey that echoes Muffat's visit backstage in Chapter 1. Like Muffat, Pepys is disconcerted by his experience of the backstage world, not least when he comes across the theatrical detritus of leftover costumes and props, now lying desolate and unused, seeing:

> here a wooden-leg, there a ruff, here a hobby-horse, there a crown [that] would make a man split himself to see with laughing. And particularly Lacy's wardrobe, and Shotrell's. But then again, to think how fine they show on the stage by candle-light, and how poor things they are to look at now too near hand, is not pleasant at all.
>
> (Pepys, 1991, p. 149)

Pepys's laughter quickly turns to melancholy and even introspection. The objects that have lived for him on the stage, the costumes that once appeared so beautiful, now seem poor and abject in the cold light of day. What was for Pepys a living breathing body in performance is now a dismembered set of objects, and the actors Lacy and Shotrell haunt the costumes that were once so crucial for producing their presence on the stage. For Pepys, the objects of costume had a theatrical life, and he mourns its loss.

Pepys is moved to melancholy when he sees the peculiar status of costumes after the performance has ended. However, of course, the objects do not lose their life completely. Pepys continues to ascribe the costumes with characteristics that do not allow them appear entirely dead. These costumes continue to resonate after the performance has ended: their presence is not mute, but rather replete with meanings and memories.The messy mix of costumes and objects, 'and what a mixture of things there was' (Pepys, 1991, p. 149), is one marked by loss, inscribed by their previous incarnation by candle-light. Perhaps for Pepys, these costumes gesture towards the impermanence and decay of appearance more generally. His response to the left-over costumes is similar to Barbara Hogdon's reaction to the Royal Shakespeare

Company archive, describing its costumes as: 'a trace of performance torn away from performance, no longer quite life, yet not dead' (Hogdon, 2006, p. 139). The un-dead qualities of the costumes after a performance has ended are telling of the larger connection between costume, deathliness and the uncanny in performance. Ghosts don't only appear onstage in armour; sometimes they haunt the theatre archive and museum in the form of leftover costume.

Costume and Memory

Costumes and props pose a particular problem for the tension between theatre's impulse to erase itself and to remember itself in subsequent performances. The question of theatre's vanishing act has been well interrogated by scholars such as Peggy Phelan (1993), Philip Auslander (1999) and Rebecca Schneider (2001). However, what have been less well documented are the memories carried on in the detritus of costumes left over after the performance has ended. The fact that costumes remain, and may be put to use in subsequent productions, sometimes in new forms, suggests that costumes act as a literally material memory of performance, permeated and formed by the work of the performer. The work may appear to disappear, but the imprint of that work, as if in a faulty wax mould, continues in the textures, smells and shapes of the fabric left behind. Costumes hanging in a wardrobe, or on a mannequin, bear the traces of a lost performance and a lost body, in their sweat marks, frayed edges, indentations of absent elbows or knees (see Hogden, 2006, pp. 135–168). These traces are clues to the past performance, and invoke the presence of something that has gone, but tell us very little about how the costume was used, and how the audience might have felt about it in the production. The costume in the archive stands as a testament to a performance that has gone but is stubbornly mute in its unwillingness to tell us "what really happened."

As Hogden points out, this stubborn muteness does not prevent theatres regularly using costume in front of house displays as evidence of past performance. However, costumes displayed on mannequins are permeated by a sense of eeriness, marked by the absence of torso, or neck, or hands. Perhaps they tell us less about the use of costume in past performance and more about costume's inherent strangeness? The costume on the mannequin confronts us with the fact that the costume *can* be taken off after all, that it is not seamless with the actor as we had thought, but is a removable object, an object with seeming autonomy and a body of its own. We thought that we had seen the actor onstage, but now we find that the actor is before us again in the archive, this time without breath or flesh or voice, but somehow still peculiarly present. We realise that what we saw onstage was not so much the actor, as the enactment of costuming: the peculiar conflation between flesh and dress and presence. The autonomy of the uninhabited costume is troubling and uncanny in Freud's sense, both familiar and strange, like a double of the thing it once was (see Freud, 2003, p. 364). It is an incomplete body, brimming with potential and memory, imprinted by a body but no longer of it and offering a ghostly and inanimate outline of a body of its own. Like Pentheus's severed head in *The Bacchae*, the leftover costume resembles a dismembered body, torn asunder by the loss of performance, having been mistaken once for something alive and of our world, something that convinced us of its verisimilitude that has now been emptied and pulled apart, its face hollow and staring.

Pepys's melancholy might come from his sense of loss after the performance has ended, but it's possible that the sadness and strangeness of unworn costumes may also be redolent of the losses inbuilt in the performance event itself, in our desires as audience members for connection and presence, and the inevitable disappointments and dislocations that the performance brings. Herbert Blau describes this feeling in *The Audience* as the: 'common experience of fracture' (cited in Auslander, 1997, pp. 56–57), which suggests that the costume is always-already empty even when worn. The actor is never quite present enough onstage, is always distanced by memories or distractions or the discomforts of being an audience member. Perhaps eeriness was always part of our experience of the costume, even when watching it onstage: the eeriness is only underlined by the blankness of the empty mask on display. The costume unworn underscores the losses that are inbuilt into the performance itself: the unknowable privacies of the actor, the fragmentary relationship between audience members, the desire for connection and its loss. Costumes exposed and disposed provoke laughter and are haunted by a sense of unease, imbued with mournfulness for the impossibility of a solace that theatre promises, but never quite fulfills. Perhaps all costumes are for ghosts in one way or another?

Of course, these eerie effects of theatrical detritus are hardly a surprise: the theatre actively harnesses the eeriness of costume all the time. One effect shared by Vawter's make-up and Schmidt's video death mask in the previous chapter was how the dead came alive onstage through the inheritance of costumes and objects in performance. The ghostly effects of this inheritance may have been foregrounded by the productions, but it's actually a typical effect of much theatre. After all, costumes are hardly automatically removed from the performance to the archive or the bin after the show is over: they are more usually retained and remade for subsequent productions. The stock theatre wardrobe has always recycled costumes from performance to performance. The theatre stock enunciates costume's peculiar status as an uncanny, removable and reusable object, bearing the weight of accumulated memories and uses from previous shows. The ghostly effects of the costume stock have been knowingly employed by companies, like the Wooster Group and Forced Entertainment, whose ongoing uses of costumes (such as blackface, Japanese robes, crap skeletons or gorilla suits) "rewards" the loyal spectator with a set of reinforced memories of past work, playing on and foregrounding the ghostly remembrance and repetition at the heart of theatre.

Furthermore, theatre's tendency to recycle has been actively harnessed by actors themselves, as a means to connect star inheritance with superstition. Barbara Hogdon tells the story of the sword that was passed from Edmund Kean to his son Henry Irving, to his daughter Kate Terry, to her son John Gielgud, who finally passed it onto his friend Laurence Olivier: 'when asked to whom he would give it, Olivier replied: "no one, it's mine," sealing off the memory's transmissions' (Hogden, 2006, p. 165). In this story, the sword becomes an embodied form of performed memory. The ability of costumes and props to make the dead present on the stage, through the costumed living actor, is at the centre of this anecdote. We can see a further belief in the power of costume in this story: it doesn't only make the dead present on the stage; it is also thought to imbue the actors who wear the inherited costume with the powers of their ancestors, situating them within a set of theatrical inheritances and legacies. Just as we saw the ghost become present through his son's body in Jonathan Pryce's Hamlet, here we see the ghosts of Kean, Irving, Terry and Gielgud emerge, in theory, not only in the sword itself, but in Olivier's performance with the sword. This is exactly the effect that Vawter tapped into in his use of Jack Smith's ashes, and the same principle that informs Kostya's discovery of "the Critic" in the old coat he finds in the theatre's wardrobe: costumes and make-up work as magic talismans in the economy of superstition and inheritance that fuels the logic of act-ing practice. The recycling and reuse of costume transmits memory, and infects and bolsters the actor's performance with the voices and bodies of the dead. The fact that actors rely so strongly on accumulated memories of previous performances through inherited costume suggests that the relation between memory, presence and loss is at the heart of the actor's work.

Costumes, then, have a peculiar half-life once a performance has ended. Cos-tumes, when they are re-used in the theatre, partly determine what modes of performance might be made possible, establishing and reiterating theatrical bodies in advance of the individual performers that might occupy them (see Diana Taylor, 2003). Costumes are an element of performance that appears to be relatively easy to retain and order after the show has ended: they seem to be a comfortingly material aspect of an ephemeral art form. However, when we actually confront this object in the archive or a front-of-house display, we can see that this idea is not strictly true: the costume has transformed itself behind our backs, turning itself into a memento of loss rather than being a reliable piece of evidence, reminding us of the strangeness of costume in performance.

While costume stubbornly resists our desire to find a safe and stable documenta-tion of a performance that has gone, we could imagine a different form of archival work that might make a new performance out of a reconstruction of the scars and stresses, the dirt and odours, of the costume itself. What would this performance look like, a performance that attempted to reconstruct what might have made those sleeves fray, or elbows bulge? What would a performance look like that investigated the bloodstains and smells and darning? This version of archival research would not in the least resemble or rediscover the performance it reconstructs through the fabric of the costumes, but after all, what attempt to reconstruct performance actually suc-ceeds? Perhaps the performance I am describing is in fact the performance we see all the time on the stage, a failed attempt at archaeology, a gesture to what is gone, a performance of memory, presence and loss that is at the heart of the relationship between the costumed actor and the audience at the theatre.

This is a book that is haunted by imaginary spectators, who have trooped through its pages, confused, melancholic and alarmed by what they see at the theatre. From Pentheus's drunken vision to Tilney's outrage and Egbert's obliteration, these spectators show us that the theatre is a disorienting place. The costumed actor is at the heart of their confusion. They are disoriented by costuming's ability to reveal the power of clothes to shape identity and form bodies. They are outraged by the fact that the audience can only gain imaginative access to actors' bodies through their clothes. They are made dizzy by the actor's ability to stand as a metaphor for the different ways to do the body: the different ways to dress. Their confusion might come from the fact that costume can reconfigure what the actor is made of, that it can redraw the boundaries of the self. It might be due to theatre revealing that the idea of the real performer onstage is the outcome of clothes. It might be because of the disappointments of nudity, the fact that nudity turns out to be a version of costuming, it might be because of the inherently ghostly qualities of costumed actors on the stage or it might be because the costume is a body without a body in the archive or museum.

In the end, Garrick's wig, Vawter's make-up, Franko's blood, Craig's ubermarionette, Valk's blackface, Kostya's coat, Viola's disguise and Mr Noaks' sword all stand for the costumed actor's surprising power to confuse, infect, entertain and enrage the audiences at the theatre. William Hazlitt called the actor 'a complicated [...] tissue of costumes' (Hazlitt, 1979, p. 43). This book has thought about the complicated experience of watching costumed actors in performance: its confusions, disorientations and pleasures. It turns out, in the end, that dressing-up produces many more ways of seeing than the double vision that Pentheus suffers in *The Bacchae*. Dressing-up is at the heart of the multiple, contradictory and uncanny visions that emerge in the exchange of looks between the costumed actor and the audience at the theatre.

Bibliography

Abel, E. (1997), 'Introduction', E. Abel, B. Christian, H. Moglen, eds. *Female Subjects in Black And White* (Berkeley: University of California Press).

Aristotle (2001) *The Basic Works of Aristotle* (New York: Random House).

Aronson, A. (2005) *Looking into the Abyss: Essays on Scenography* (Ann Arbor: University of Michigan Press).

Arnott, P. (1959) *An Introduction to the Greek Theatre* (London: Macmillan).

Artaud, A. (1970) *The Theatre and its Double* (London: Caldar & Boyars).

Auslander, P. (1997) *From Acting to Performance: Essays in Modernism and Postmodernism* (London: Routledge).

Auslander, P. (1999) *Liveness: Performances in a Mediatized Culture* (London: Routledge).

Auslander, P. (ed.) (2003) *Performance: Critical Concepts in Literary and Cultural Studies* (London: Routledge).

Balla, G. (2000) 'The Antineutral Dress, A Futurist Manifesto', in U. Lehmann, ed. *Tigersprung: Fashion in Modernity* (Cambridge: MIT Press).

Barthes, R. (1982) 'Striptease', S. Sontag ed. *Barthes; Selected Writings* (Oxford: Fontana).

Barthes, R. (2000) *Camera Lucida: Reflections on Photography* (London: Vintage).

Baugh, C. (2004) 'Stage Designs from Lutherberg to Poel', J. Milling, P. Thompson, J. Donohue, B. Kershaw eds. *Cambridge History of British Theatre* (Cambridge: Cambridge University Press).

Baugh, C. (2005) *Theatre, Performance, Technology: The Development of Scenography in the Twentieth Century* (Basingstoke: Palgrave Macmillan).

Beckett, S. (1986) *The Complete Dramatic Works* (London: Faber & Faber).

Bennett, S. (1997) *Theatre Audiences: A Theory of Production & Reception* (London: Routledge).

Berghaus, G. (2005) *Theatre, Performance and the Historical Avant-Garde* (Basingstoke & New York: Palgrave Macmillan).

Bergson, H. (2008) *Laughter: An Essay on the Meaning of the Comic* (London: Dodo Press).

Bernhardt, S. (1889) 'Sarah Bernhardt and Hamlet: Interesting Letter', *Daily Telegraph* (London), 17th June.

Bhabha, H. K. (1994) *The Location of Culture* (London: Routledge).

Bicat, T. (2001) *Making Stage Costumes: A Practical Guide* (Marlborough: Crowood Press).

Billington, M. (1989) *Country Life* (London), 5th January.

Billington, M. (1994) 'Great Danes' *The Guardian*, 2nd November.

Blue Blouse (1995) 'Simple Advice to Participants', R. Drain ed. *Twentieth Century Theatre: A Sourcebook* (London: Routledge).

Booth, M. (1965) *English Melodrama* (London: H. Jenkins).

Booth, M. (1991) *Theatre in the Victorian Age* (Cambridge: Cambridge University Press).

Braun, E. (1969) *Meyerhold on Theatre* (London: Methuen).

Brecht, B. (1955) *Mother Courage and her Children* (New York: Grove Press).

Brown, G. (1995) *The Independent* (London) 26th May.

Butler, J. (1993) *Bodies That Matter: On the Discursive Limits of "Sex"* (New York: Routledge).

Butler, J. (1999) *Gender Trouble: Feminism and the Subversion of Identity* (New York: Routledge).

Cambridge (2009) *Cambridge Advanced Learner's Dictionary*, http://dictionary.cambridge.org/define.asp?key=41847& dict=CALD (first accessed, 06-04-2009).

Carlson, M. (2001) *The Haunted Stage: Theatre as Memory Machine* (Ann Arbor: University of Michigan Press).

Carter, M. (2003) *Fashion Classics: From Carlyle to Barthes* (Berg Publishers).

Chekhov, A. (1997) 'Three Sisters', P. Schmidt trans., *The Plays of Anton Chekhov* (New York: Harper Collins).

Chronacher, K. (1992) 'Unmasking the Minstrel Mask's Black Magic in Ntozake Shange's *Spell #7*', *Theatre Journal*, Vol. 44, No. 2, 177–195.

Clark, K. (1956) *The Nude: A Study of Ideal Art* (Harmondsworth: Penguin).

Coen, S. (1997) 'The Fascination of What's Difficult', *American Theatre*, Vol. 14, No. 3, 12–17.

Corns, T. (2007) *A History of Seventeenth Century English Literature* (Malden: Wiley-Blackwell).

Craig, E. G. (1911) 'The Actor and the Uber-Marionette', *On the Art of the Theatre* (London: William Heineman).

Craig, E. G. (1984) 'A Note on Masks', J. M. Walton ed. *Craig on Theatre* (London: Methuen).

Dekker, T. (1979) *The Shoemaker's Holiday: A Pleasant Comedy of the Gentle Craft* (Manchester: Manchester University Press).

Delaunay, S. (2000) 'Artists and the future of Fashion', in U. Lehmann, ed. *Tigersprung: Fashion in Modernity* (Cambridge: MIT Press).

Dolan, J. (1998) 'The Discourse of Feminisms: The Spectator and Representation', L. Goodman and J. de Gay eds. *The Routledge Reader in Gender and Performance* (London & New York: Routledge).

Downes, J. (1708) 'Roscius Anglicanus', J. McCollum ed. *The Restoration Stage* (Connecticut: Greenwood Press).

Edwardes, J. (1989) *Time Out* (London), 4th January.

Eisenstein, S. (1995) 'The Montage of Attractions', R. Drain ed. *Twentieth Century Theatre: A Sourcebook* (London: Routledge).

Entwistle, J. (2000) *The Fashioned Body: Fashion, Dress and Modern Social Theory* (Cambridge: Polity Press).

Etchells, T. (2008) 'When an Actor Plays Dead no one's Fooled for a Moment', *Spectacular Programme* (London: Forced Entertainment/Riverside Studios).

Esslin, M. (1978) *The Field of Drama: How the Signs of Drama Create Meaning on Stage and Screen* (London: Methuen).

Esslin, M. (1980) *The Theatre of the Absurd* (Harmondsworth: Penguin).

Euripides (1954) *The Bacchae and other Plays* (London: Penguin).

Ferris, L. (1993) *Crossing the Stage: Controversies on Cross-Dressing* (London: Routledge).

Foakes, R. A. (2005) 'Armed at Point Exactly: The Ghost in Hamlet', *Shakespeare Survey*, Vol. 58, 34–48.

Foley, B. (2005) *Undressed for Success: Beauty Contestants and Exotic Dancers as Merchants of Morality* (Basingstoke & New York: Palgrave Macmillan).

Forced Entertainment (2004) *Bloody Mess* (Dublin & London: DVD).

Franko, B. (1998) 'Body Art', *The Southbank Show* (London).

French, S. (1991) 'Parts Others Cannot Reach', *Independent on Sunday* (London) 1st September.

Freud, S. (2003) *The Uncanny* (London: Penguin).

Gannon, L. (2007) 'You can't live at that level', *The Guardian*, 30th March.

Globe (1899) 'Mdme Bernhardt's *"Hamlet"* ', *The Globe* (London), 13th June.

Gordon, A. (1997) *Ghostly Matters: Haunting and the Sociological Imagination* (Minneapolis & London: University of Minnesota Press).

Gosson, S. (1582) 'Plays Confuted in Five Actions', in A. F. Kinney ed. (1974), *Markets of Bawdrie: The Dramatic Criticism of Stephen Gosson* (Salzburg: Institut für Englische Spräche und Literature).

Graver, D. (2003), 'The Actor's Bodies', Phillip Auslander ed. *Performance*, Vol. 2 (London: Routledge), pp. 157–175

Graves Miller, J. (2007) *Ariane Mnouchkine* (London: Routledge).

Halliday, F. E. (1964) *A Shakespeare Companion 1564–1964*. (Baltimore: Penguin).

Halliday, F. E. (1969) *A Shakspeare Companion* (Harmondsworth: Penguin).

Hamlet Playbill (1742), Drury Lane Theatre (London), 17th November.

Harris, J. (1992) *Medieval Theatre in Context: An Introduction* (London: Routledge).

Hazlitt, W. (1957) 'On Actors and Acting', W. Archer and R. Lowe ed. *Hazlitt on Theatre* (New York: Hill & Wang).

Hazlitt, W. (1979) 'On Actors and Acting', A. Hinchliffe ed. *Drama Criticism – Developments since Ibsen* (Basingstoke: Macmillan).

Halliburton, R. (2000) 'It's a Bleeding Liberty', *The Independent on Sunday*, 26th April.

Hinsliff, G. (2005) 'Blair's Blushes Merely Cosmetic', *The Observer*, 24th July.

Garber, M. (1993) *Vested Interests: Cross-Dressing and Cultural Diversity* (Harmondsworth: Penguin).

Greenblat, S. (2001) *Hamlet in Purgatory* (Princeton & Oxford: Princeton University Press).

Govan, F. (2005) 'Blair's Make-up Bill Runs to $1, 800', *The Telegraph* (London), 25th July.

Hoffman, B. (2006) '*Bloody Mess*, Theatre Reviews', *Theatre Journal*, Vol. 58, No. 4, 701–703.

Hogdon, B. (2006) 'Shopping in the Archive: Material Memories', in P. Hollander ed. *Shakespeare, Memory and Performance* (Cambridge: Cambridge University Press), pp. 135–168.

Hollander, A. (1993) *Seeing Through Clothes* (Berkeley: University of California Press).

Hornby, R. (1996) 'Richard II', *The Hudson Review*, Winter.

Hutton, J. (2003) *Fashionable Follies: A Comedy in Five Acts* (Cambridge: Cambridge University Press).

IMDB (2002) 'Matt Damon's Stage Fury', http://www.imdb.com/news/wenn/2002-06-13 (accessed 10-4-2008).

Ignatiev, N. (1995) *How the Irish Became White in America* (New York: Routledge).

Jardine, L. (1983) *Still Harping on Daughters: Women and Drama in the Age of Shakespeare* (Sussex: Harvester Press).

Jones, A. (2006) 'Corporeal Malediction: Franko B's Body/Art and the Trace of Whiteness, http://www.franko-b.com/text5.htm, (accessed Thursday, 10th April, 2008).

Jones, A. R. & Stallybrass, P. (2000) *Renaissance Clothing and the Materials of Memory* (Cambridge: Cambridge University Press).

Kalb, J. (1998) *New York Press*, 25–31 March.

Kaplan, J. & Stowell, S. (1995) *Theatre and Fashion: Oscar Wilde to the Suffragettes* (Cambridge: Cambridge University Press).

Kastan, D. S. (1999) *A Companion to Shakespeare* (Malden: Wiley Blackwell).

Kiberd, D. (1996) *Inventing Ireland: The Literature of the Modern Nation* (London: Vintage).

Kirby, M. (1971) *Futurist Performance: Theory and Practice in the Drama, Scenography, Acting, Costumes, Film and Music of the Italian Futurists* (New York: E. P. Dutton).

Knowles, R. (2004) *Reading the Material Theatre* (Cambridge: Cambridge University Press).

Koenig, R. (1995) 'The Girl Who Would be King', *Independent* (London), 5th June.

Lamanova, N. (2000) Concerning Contemporary Dress', in U. Lehmann ed. *Tigersprung: Fashion in Modernity* (Cambridge: MIT Press).

Lott, E. (1993) *Love and Theft, Blackface Minstrelsy and the American Working Class* (Oxford: Oxford University Press).

Laver, J. (1964) *Costume in the Theatre* (London: Harrap).

Lichte, E. (1992) *The Semiotics of Theater* (Bloomington: Indiana University Press).

Lyall, S. (2007) 'The Tale of Harry Potter and the Naked Role', *The New York Times*, 7th March.

Daily Mail (1899) 'A Woman's Hamlet: How Mme Bernhardt Studied the Part', *Daily Mail*, (London), 13th June.

Melrose, S. (1994) *A Semiotics of the Dramatic Text* (Basingstoke: Macmillan).

Mayakovsky, V. (1968) 'Mystery Bouffe', *The Complete Plays of Vladimir Mayakovsky* (New York: Simon and Schuster).

McClintock, A. (1995) *Imperial Leather, Race, Gender and Sexuality in Colonial Contest* (New York: Routledge).

McFerran, A. (1994) 'Best Feet Forward', *Evening Standard* (London), 10 March.

Melzer, A. (1994) *Dada and Surrealist Performance* (Baltimore: Johns Hopkins University Press).

Meyerhold, V. (1995) 'The Reconstruction of the Theatre', R. Drain ed. *Twentieth Century Theatre: A Sourcebook* (London: Routledge).

Meyerhold, V. (1972) 'A Theatre for Meyerhold', Braun, Edward trans. *Theatre Quarterly*, Vol. II, No. 7, July–September, 69–73.

Monks, A. (2008) 'Interview with Samuel West', Unpublished manuscript.

Mulvey, L. (1998) 'Visual Pleasure and Narrative Cinema', L. Goodman & J. de Gay eds. *The Routledge Reader in Gender and Performance* (London & New York: Routledge).

Nead, L. (1992) *The Female Nude: Art, Obscenity and Sexuality* (London: Routledge).

Norman, M. & Stoppard, T. (1999) *Shakespeare in Love: Screenplay* (London: Faber & Faber).

O'Neill, E. (1998) 'The Emperor Jones', *Four Plays by Eugene O'Neill* (New York: Signet Classic).

O'Toole, F. (2008) 'Revealing New Details in a Stunning New Production of "Happy Days", *The Irish Times* (Dublin), 'Weekend Section', 11th October, http://www.irishtimes.com/newspaper/weekend/2008/1011/1223560388307.html (first accessed 06-04-2009).

O'Toole, F. (2000) *Irish Theatre Magazine*, Vol. 2, No. 6, Summer.

Orgel, S. (1975) *The Illusion of Power: Political Theatre in the English Renaissance* (Berkeley: University of California Press).

Pepys, S. (1991) 'Diary', in J. McCollum ed. *The Restoration Stage* (Connecticut: Greenwood Press).

Peter, J. (1991) *The Sunday Times* (London), 30th June.

Phelan, P. (1993) *Unmarked: The Politics of Performance* (London & New York: Routledge).

Potter, L. (2002) *Othello* (Manchester: Manchester University Press).

Price, C. (1973), *Theatre in the Age of Garrick* (Oxford: Basil Blackwell).

Puchner, M. (2002) *Stage Fright: Modernism, Anti-Theatricality and Drama* (Baltimore: Johns Hopkins University Press).

Quinn, M. (1990) 'Celebrity and the Semiotics of Acting', *New Theatre Quarterly*, Vol. 6, No. 22, 154–161.

Ridout, N. (2006) *Stage Fright, Animals and other Theatrical Problems* (Cambridge: Cambridge University Press).

Roach, J. (1993) *The Player's Passion: Studies in the Science of Acting* (Ann Arbor: Michigan University Press).

Roediger, D. (1991) *The Wages of Whiteness, Race and the Making of the American Working Class* (London: Verso).

Rutter, C. C. (1997) 'Fiona Shaw's Richard II: The Girl as Player-King as Comic', *Shakespeare Quarterly*, Vol. 48, No. 3, 314–324.

Savran, D. (1988) *Breaking the Rules, the Wooster Group* (New York: Theatre Communications Group).

Schechner, R. (1998) 'Ron Vawter: For the Record', H. Hughes and D. Roman eds. *O Solo Homo: The New Queer Performance* (New York: Grove Press).

Schneider, R. (2001) 'Performance Remains', *Performance Research*, Vol. 6, No. 2, 100–108.

Schulz, D. V. (1999) 'The Architecture of Conspicuous Consumption: Property, Class, and Display at Herbert Beerbohm Tree's Her Majesty's Theatre', *Theatre Journal*, Vol. 51, No. 3, 231–250.

Segal, C. (1982) *Dionysiac Poetics and Euripides' Bacchae* (Princeton: Princeton University Press).

Senelick, L. (2000) *The Changing Room: Sex, Drag and Theatre* (London: Routledge).

Sennett, R. (1976) *The Fall of Public Man* (London: Penguin).

Shange, N. (1991) *Plays One: Notzake Shange* (London: Methuen).

Shaw, G. B. (1957) *Major Barbara* (London: Penguin).

Simmel, G. (1997) *Simmel on Culture*, D. Frisby & M. Featherstone ed. (London: Sage Publications).

Simon, J. (1996) 'Of Poets and Puppets', *New York Magazine* (New York), 9 December.

Solomon, A. (1997) *Redressing the Canon: Essays on Theatre and Gender* (London: Routledge).

Spencer, C. (1995) 'King on the Verge of a Breakdown', *Daily Telegraph* (London), 5 June.

Spencer, C. (2002) 'Top Five Theatrical Sex Scenes', *The Telegraph*, 31 August.

Stanislavski, C. (2001) *Building a Character* (London: Methuen).

States, B. (1985) *Great Reckonings in Little Rooms: On the Phenomenology of Theatre* (Berkeley, London: University of California Press).

States, B. (2003) 'Performance as Metaphor', P. Auslander ed. *Performance*, Vol. 1 (London: Routledge), pp. 108–138.

Steen, S. (2000) 'Melancholy Bodies: Racial Subjectivity and Whiteness in O'Neill's *The Emperor Jones*', *Theatre Journal*, Vol. 52, No. 2, 100–108.

Stubbes, P. (1973) *The Anatomie of Abuses* (New York: Garland Press).

Sutcliffe, P. (2006) 'A Thrill that is Barely Concealed', *The Independent*, 29 September.

Suvin, D. (1967) 'Beckett's Purgatory of the Individual or the 3 Laws of Thermodynamics: Notes for an Incamination towards a Presubluminary Exagmination Round Beckett's Factification', *Tulane Drama Review*, Vol. 11, No. 4, Summer.

Taylor, D. (2003) *The Archive and the Repertoire: Performing Cultural Memory in the Americas* (Durham & London: Duke University Press).

Temple, A. (1995) 'To Play the King (and be a Woman)', *Independent* (London), 21 May.

Toepfer, K. (1996) 'Nudity and Textuality in Postmodern Performance', *Performing Arts Journal*, Vol. 54, No. 18.3, 76–91.

Twain, M. (2003) 'Reminiscences', R. Lewis ed. *From Travelling Show to Vaudeville: Theatrical Spectacle in America, 1830–1910* (Baltimore: Johns Hopkins University Press).

Veblen, T. (1994) *The Theory of the Leisure Class* (New York: Dover).

Volt (Vincenzo Fani) (2000) 'Futurist Manifesto of Women's Fashion', Lehmann, U. ed. *Tigersprung: Fashion in Modernity* (Cambridge: MIT Press).

Wainscott, R. H. (1988) *Staging O'Neill: The Experimental Years, 1920–1934* (New Haven: Yale University Press).

Wardle, I. (1988) *The Times* (London), 22 December.

Wells, H. G. (1913) 'The Obliterated Man', *The Literature Network* www.online-literature.com/wellshg/2873/, (accessed 29-11-08).

West End Whingers (2007) 'Review: Equus with Daniel Radcliffe', http://westend whingers.wordpress.com/2007/03/20/review-equus-with-daniel-radcliffe, (accessed 29-11-08).

Wharton, E. (1994) *The Age of Innocence* (London: Wordsworth).

Wilde, O. (2000) 'Slaves of Fashion', in U. Lehmann ed. *Tigersprung: Fashion in Modernity* (Cambridge: MIT Press).

The Wooster Group (2003) *Brace Up!* (New York: St Anne's Warehouse), March.

Wycherley, T. (2001) *The Country Wife* (London: Nick Hern Books).

Zarrilli, P. (2002) *Acting Reconsidered: A Theoretical and Practical Guide* (London: Routledge).

Zola, E. (1992) *Nana* (Oxford & New York: Oxford University Press).

Index